Windows NT Workstation User's Guide

George Eckel

New Riders

New Riders Publishing, Indianapolis, Indiana

Windows NT Workstation User's Guide

By George Eckel

Published by:
New Riders Publishing
201 West 103rd Street
Indianapolis, IN 46290 USA

Printed in the United States of America 1 2 3 4 5 6 7 8 9 0

CIP data available upon request

Warning and Disclaimer

This book is designed to provide information about Windows NT Workstation. Every effort has been made to make this book as complete and as accurate as possible, but no warranty or fitness is implied.

The information is provided on an "as is" basis. The author(s) and New Riders Publishing shall have neither liability nor responsibility to any person or entity with respect to any loss or damages arising from the information contained in this book or from the use of the disks or programs that may accompany it.

Publisher *Don Fowley*
Publishing Manager *Emmett Dulaney*
Marketing Manager *Mary Foote*
Managing Editor *Carla Hall*

Development Editor
Ian Sheeler
Project Editor
Laura Frey
Copy Editor
David Bradford
Associate Marketing Manager
Tamara Apple
Acquisitions Coordinator
Stacia Mellinger
Publisher's Assistant
Karen Opal
Cover Designer
Sandra Schroeder
Book Designer
Sandra Schroeder
Manufacturing Coordinator
Brook Farling
Production Manager
Kelly Dobbs
Production Team Supervisor
Laurie Casey
Graphic Image Specialists
Clint Lahnen
Laura Robbins
Craig Small
Todd Wente
Production Team
Heather Butler
Angela Calvert
Kim Cofer
Tricia Flodder
David Garratt
Erika Millen
Beth Rago
Erich Richter
Christine Tyner
Karen Walsh
Indexers
Ginny Bess
John Hulse
Production Analysts
Jason Hand
Bobbi Satterfield

About the Author

George Eckel has worked on a number of books for Macmillan Publishing, including *Memory Management for All of Us*, *Inside Windows NT*, and *Inside Unix*. As a professional writer, George has worked as a consultant for Hewlett-Packard, Sun Microsystems, Informix, AT&T, Time-Warner, and Silicon Graphics, Inc. Presently, he is part of the core team that developed and demonstrated the world's first interactive television, and is running a consulting business for companies setting up services on the Internet. You can reach him at geckel@warp.engr.sgi.com, or 510-820-5243.

George is the father to three children: Madeline, Nathalie, and Genevieve, and happy husband of Shirlee, whose patience and support helped make this book possible.

Trademark Acknowledgments

Acknowledgments

George Eckel would like to thank everyone who worked so hard to make this book possible.

Contents at a Glance

Table of Contents

CHAPTER 1

Exploring Windows NT New Interface

Since the inception of Windows NT, the NT interface has resembled the Windows 3.*x* interface. Windows NT always had more applets, such as Scheduler+, than Windows 3.*x*, but the look of the interfaces was the same. The similarity was intentional; users of one operating system found it easy to switch to the other.

The latest version of Windows, Windows 95, employs a dramatically different interface from Windows 3.1. Windows NT adopts the same interface in version 4.0. In Windows NT, the interface is called Windows NT Explorer.

The main difference between the Windows NT 3.*x* and Windows NT 4.0 interface is the use of the desktop metaphor. In version 3.*x*, applications and devices were grouped into application groups. You could move an application icon from one group to another, but you could not, for example, move an icon out of the Program Manager onto the wallpaper.

Windows NT Explorer dispenses with Program Manager. In Explorer, you can display files, applications, directories, and devices (such as printers) as icons on the root window, which is the wallpaper. Liberating application and device icons from application groups gives you more direct access to these objects; it also enables you to fill the desktop (the root window) with all of the tools you commonly need to accomplish your tasks.

Windows NT Explorer presents a radically new interface to the user. After you start an application, however, everything works just about the same as it did in version 3.*x*. So, although the new interface might at first be a shock, once you get familiar with finding application and device icons, and get familiar with placing them on the desktop, your biggest learning hurdle is over. Perhaps the only other novelty is getting used to using two mouse buttons on a regular basis rather than just one.

This chapter describes the Windows NT Explorer interface.

Getting Windows NT Explorer for Version 3.51

If you are running Windows NT version 3.51, you can download the Windows NT Explorer and duplicate most of what Windows NT version 4.0 has to offer. To download the Windows NT Explorer, use the anonymous FTP server at Microsoft and download one of the following files, according to the platform you are running:

For Intel platforms:

`ftp://ftp.microsoft.com/bussys/winnt/winnt-unsup-ed/newshell/nt351nsi.exe`

For Alpha platforms:

`ftp://ftp.microsoft.com/bussys/winnt/winnt-unsup-ed/newshell/nt351nsa.exe`

For PowerPC:

`ftp://ftp.microsoft.com/bussys/winnt/winnt-unsup-ed/newshell/nt351nsp.exe`

For MIPS:

`ftp://ftp.microsoft.com/bussys/winnt/winnt-unsup-ed/newshell/nt351nsm.exe`

Note If you are unfamiliar with FTP, you can use a World Wide Web (WWW) browser to open the following URL:

```
http://www.microsoft.com
```

From Microsoft's home page, click on the following hyperlinks:

```
Microsoft Products
Microcoft Backoffice and Windows NT
Microsoft Windows NT Workstation
Windows NT Shell Technology Preview
```

The final hyperlink presents you with a list of platforms, including PowerPC, Alpha, MIPS, and x86. When you click on the hyperlink corresponding to your platform, the hyperlink starts an ftp transfer of Explorer to your system.

Alternatively, you can use the following procedure to retrieve the file using FTP:

```
% ftp ftp.microsoft.com
Connected to ftp.microsoft.com
220 sizzle.asd.sgi.com FTP server (Version 4.2.321.2 Wed Feb 15
03:24:32 GMT 1995) ready.
Name (ftp.microsoft.com:clinton): anonymous
331 Guest login ok. Use email address as password
Password: clinton@washington.com
230 Guest login ok, access restrictions apply
ftp> cd /bussys/winnt/winnt-unsup-ed/newshell
250 CWD successful
ftp> get nt351nsi.exe
200 PORT command successful
150 Opening BINARY mode data connection for nt351nsi.exe
226 Transfer complete.
ftp> quit
221 Goodbye.
>
```

This procedure downloads Windows NT Explorer for the Intel platform.

The NT Shell that you download expands to a little over 20 MB. Make sure your hard disk has enough room to handle the uncompressed files.

To install the Windows NT Explorer, run the shupdate.cmd program residing under the directory corresponding to your computer's platform. If, for example, your machine uses a 486 or Pentium processor, use the shupdate.cmd file in the I386 directory. When you reboot your computer, shupdate.cmd converts a number of files to the new format and then displays Windows NT Explorer!

You should bear in mind, however, that shupdate.cmd is beta software. The purpose of publicizing the software is for developers to integrate Explorer into their Windows NT applications and report bugs to Microsoft. Windows NT Explorer at this point is very dependable. Do not be surprised, however, to happen upon some real problems. (My display, for example, occasionally flickers.) Being able to use the Explorer interface is probably worth the risk, however. To minimize your exposure to buggy code, make sure to get the latest version of shupdate.cmd at least once a month.

Using the Root Window

If you have run Windows 3.*x* or Windows NT 3.*x*, you have become very familiar with Program Manager. Program Manager is the window in which all of your application groups appear. Starting an application was as simple as double-clicking on one of the icons in an application group. Application icons could not exist outside application groups, and application icons could not be moved outside Program Manager.

Get ready for a shock. Program Manager is gone. Now, when you log on to Windows NT, you are greeted by the root window, as shown in figure 1.1.

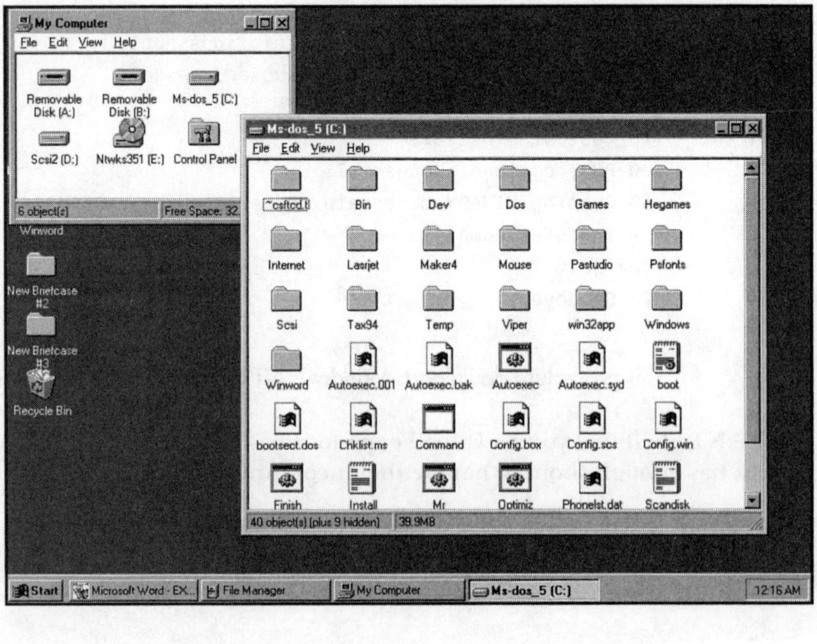

Figure 1.1

The root window of Windows NT Explorer.

Once in the root window, you see the following three icons:

- My Computer
- Network Neighborhood
- Recycle Bin

Double-clicking on the My Computer icon opens an application group that includes an icon representing the familiar Control Panel application group, and an icon representing each storage medium on your computer. For example, if you have an IDE hard drive, a SCSI hard drive, and a CD-ROM, there would be an icon for each drive. If you double-click on any of the device icons, Explorer displays the files and folders on it.

Notice that Explorer dispenses with displaying the familiar hierarchical relationships between files and directories. Instead, Explorer displays files and folders on a desktop. Folders can contain files and other folders. Double-clicking on a folder opens it, and the contents of the folder are displayed in the window.

Double-clicking on the Network Neighborhood icon opens an application group whose applications facilitate using your computer on a network. If you did not install the networking software, the application group is empty.

The Recycle Bin is a '90s twist on the familiar trash can icon. To delete applications from the desktop, just pull them into the Recycle Bin.

Double-clicking on the Recycle Bin reveals the objects that have been deleted from the desktop. They appear in a window whose menus and menu choices are similar to those found in File Manager. You have the option of using a mouse to drag objects out of the Recycle Bin to replace them on the desktop, or you can delete them for good by using options in the File menu.

Using the Root Menu

When you clicked on the wallpaper in version 3.*x*, nothing happened. When you click on the wallpaper in Explorer with the secondary mouse button, the pop-up root menu displays, as shown in figure 1.2.

The options of the root menu have the following functions:

- **Arrange Icons.** Enables you to arrange the icons on the Root window by Name, Type, Size, or Date. You can also click on the last option, Auto Arrange, to rearrange the icons automatically. Clicking on this option toggles it on or off. Leaving it checked (on) places the icons on a grid; otherwise, icons can get placed on top of one another, and a great many jumbled icons can be difficult to read.

Figure 1.2

The Root menu.

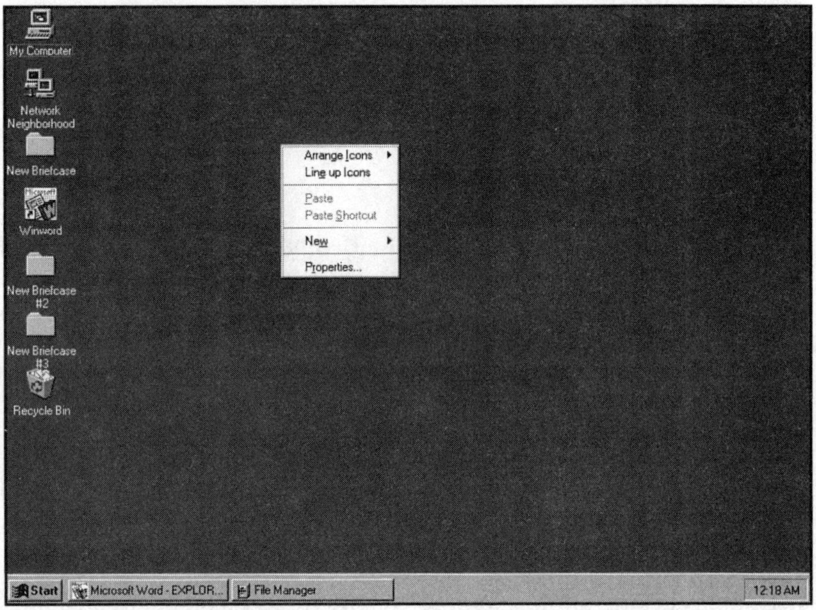

- **Line up Icons.** Positions the icons in the Root window in straight rows and columns. This is the manual equivalent to what Auto Arrange, under the Arrange Icons option, does automatically.

- **Paste.** Enables you to paste into the Root window an icon you previously cut from somewhere else. For example, if you double-click on the Recycle Bin icon, highlight one of the files in the Bin, then use the Cut option in the Edit menu to remove the highlighted file (and place it on the Clipboard), you can then use the Paste option, in the Root pop-up window, to paste the cut file into the Root window.

- **Paste Shortcut.** Enables you to paste a shortcut into the Root window. A shortcut is actually a link to an application. It appears as an icon in the Root window. Instead of using the Start button to execute applications, you can just as easily paste the icon of an application or device on the Root window so that you can double-click on it very easily to start the application.

- **Undo Delete.** Retrieves the last icon placed in the Recycle Bin and places it back on the Root window.

- **New.** Enables you to place new items in the Root window, including the following:
    - **Folder.** Places a new, empty folder in the Root window.
    - **Shortcut.** Enables you to define a Shortcut for the application in the active window. A Shortcut is a link to an application; it appears as an icon. When you double-click on it, the associated application starts. Creating a shortcut for an application is the only way to place the icon of an application on the Root window.
    - **Briefcase.** Places a briefcase icon on the Root window.
    - **Paintbrush Picture.** Displays the paint program familiar to Windows 3.*x* users.
    - **Text Document.** Places a text icon in the Root window. When you double-click on the new icon, called New Text document, Windows NT displays a window of the Notebook application included in the Windows NT software distribution. In that window you can use the Open option under the File menu to link the New Text Document icon to the opened document.
    - **Sound.** Places a sound icon in the Root window. The sound icon must represent a sound file. When you double-click on the new icon, called New Sound, Windows NT displays a window in which you can specify the pathname and filename of the sound file.
- **Properties.** Displays the Color window, which enables you to choose the colors used for the text, scroll bars, title bars, panes, and menus in all windows.

These tools enable you to create, delete, color, and name any icon that appears on the root window.

Using Shortcuts

When you click on New in the Root pop-up window and the Shortcut option in the sub pop-up window, Explorer displays the Create Shortcut window, as shown in figure 1.3.

In the text entry field, type the pathname and the name of the application or device you want direct access to. After you click on the Next button, Explorer lets you confirm your selection by clicking on the Finish or Back button to approve or disapprove the selection.

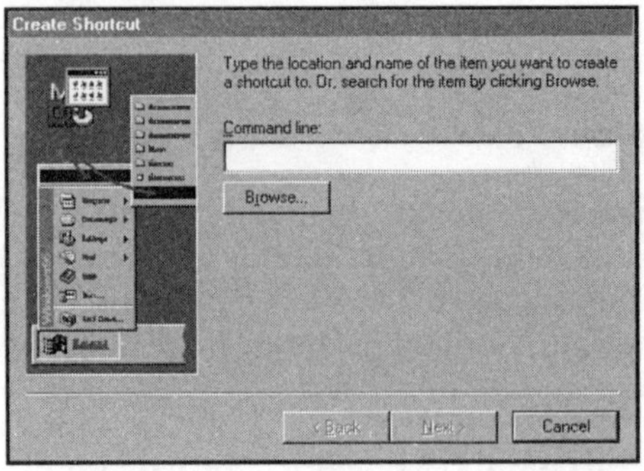

Figure 1.3
Creating a shortcut.

Using Briefcase

More and more people are using more than one computer to work on the same set of files. You might, for example, have a workstation and use a laptop computer for sales trips. Transferring files from one computer to another can lead to problems, such as overwriting the latest version of the file with an older version, or working on two instances of a file at the same time, which then requires that you somehow fit together the two differently revised files.

The Briefcase application takes the confusion out of this process. When you double-click on the briefcase icon for the first time, Windows NT Explorer displays the Welcome to the Windows Briefcase window, as shown in figure 1.4. This window explains how to use Briefcase.

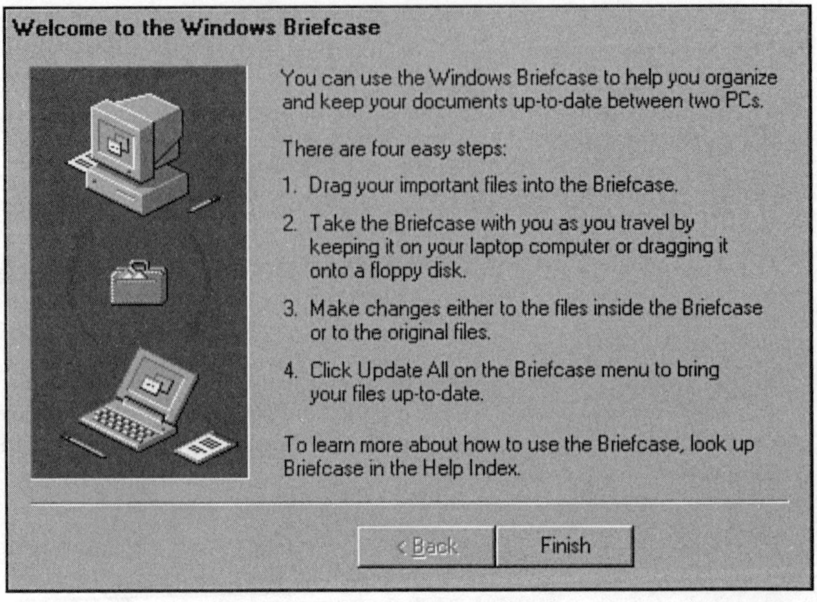

Figure 1.4
Welcome to the Windows Briefcase window.

To use Briefcase, use the following procedure:

1. Drag (or Open) files that you want to work on with more than one computer into the Briefcase window, as shown in figure 1.5.

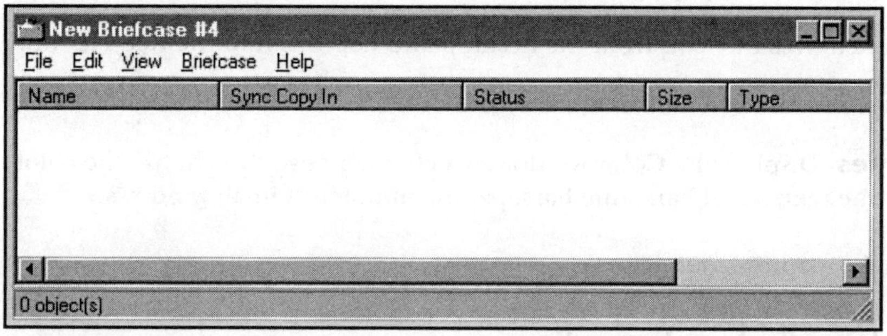

Figure 1.5
Manipulating Files in the Briefcase.

2. Keep a Briefcase on both your workstation and your other computer. To transfer all Briefcase files to a second computer by using a floppy disk, drag the Briefcase icon onto the floppy icon.
3. Work either on the files listed in the Briefcase or on the original files.
4. When you finish working on a file, use the secondary mouse button to click on the Briefcase icon. Explorer displays the icon window.
5. On the pop-up menu, click on Update All.

This option makes sure both computer systems have the latest versions of a file.

Using Icon Pop-Up Menus

When you click on an icon with the secondary mouse button, Windows NT Explorer displays an icon pop-up menu. The options on the menu vary according to the type of object the icon represents. The following list describes the common menu items:

- **Open.** Opens the window of the application that was minimized. This menu option is the equivalent of double-clicking on the icon with the primary mouse button.
- **Explore.** Used with document holders only, such as folders and briefcases, Explore shows the contents of the object in a display similar to the File Manager.
- **Cut.** Removes the icon from the Root window and places a copy of it on the Clipboard so that you can later paste it somewhere.

- **Copy.** Saves a copy of the icon to the Clipboard so that you can later paste it somewhere.
- **Create Shortcut.** Displays a new icon that is a shortcut to the icon you clicked on to display the icon pop-up menu.
- **Delete.** Removes the icon from the desktop and deposits it in the Recycle Bin.
- **Rename.** Enables you to rename the icon.
- **Properties.** Displays the Color window, which enables you to choose the colors used for the text, scroll bars, title bars, panes, and menus in all windows.

These tools make manipulating icons easy.

Recovering from Broken Applications

If you are coming from the Windows 3.*x* environment, you are already familiar with the problems of broken applications. You may have started an application and waited awhile until you realized the application was frozen. In Windows 3.*x*, the only way to recover was by pressing Ctrl+Alt+Del. Rebooting your computer meant that you had to reopen all of the applications you were running before the application crash.

Windows NT is wonderful in this regard. When an application crashes, you again press Ctrl+Alt+Del, but instead of rebooting, Windows NT returns you to the root window with the crashed application represented as an icon. The title to the icon says that the application is frozen.

When you click on the icon with the secondary mouse button, Windows NT displays the pop-up menu. You most commonly want to use the option that terminates the frozen application. (If you use the primary mouse button to click on the icon, you return to the frozen application.) When you terminate the application, the icon disappears—and that is all there is to it! No rebooting the system and reopening your applications.

Using the Taskbar

At the bottom of the root window is a bar called the Taskbar, as shown in figure 1.6.

There are four sections to the Taskbar:

- The middle part of the Taskbar, which is blank.
- On the far right side of the Taskbar, Explorer can display a digital clock.

- In the middle of the bar, buttons display for each running application. When you minimize an application, you can maximize it by clicking on its button in the Taskbar.
- On the very left of the Taskbar is the Start button, which enables you to start applications.

Figure 1.6
The Taskbar appears even when other applications are running.

This section describes the Taskbar in detail.

Setting the Display

Explorer enables you to arrange the windows in the Root window automatically. When you use the secondary mouse button to click on the part of the Taskbar that is blank, Explorer displays a pop-up menu, as shown in figure 1.7.

The options in the menu have the following definitions:

- **Cascade.** Arranges windows on top of one another, as shown in figure 1.8.
- **Tile Vertically.** Arranges windows next to one another without any overlap, as shown in figure 1.9.

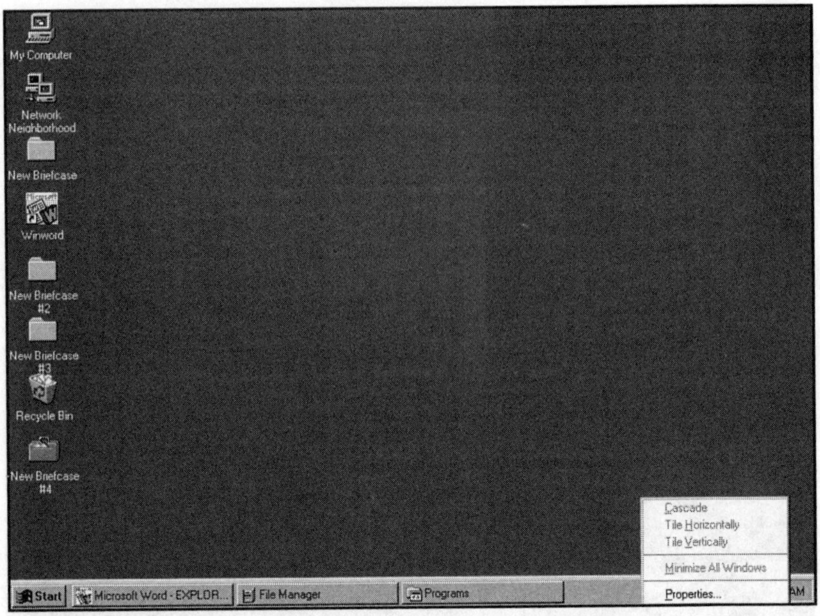

Figure 1.7
The Taskbar pop-up menu.

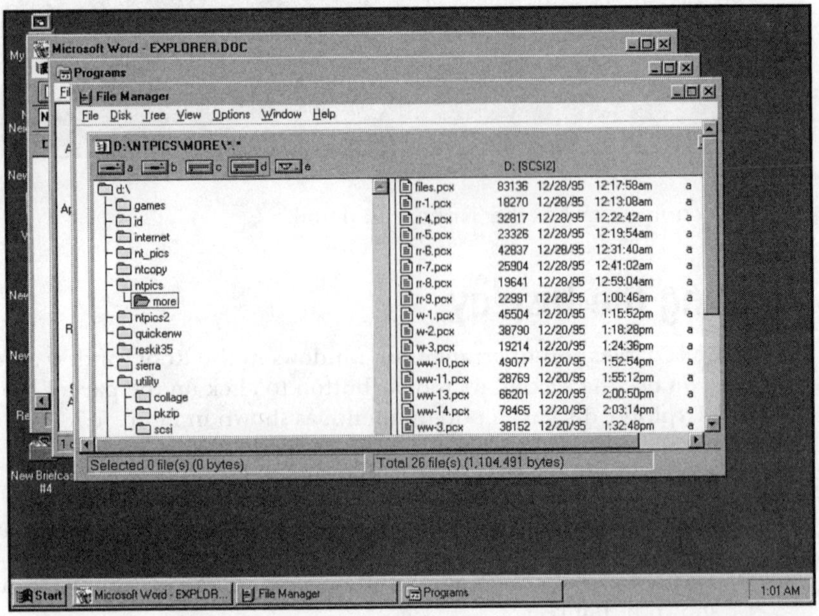

Figure 1.8
Cascading windows.

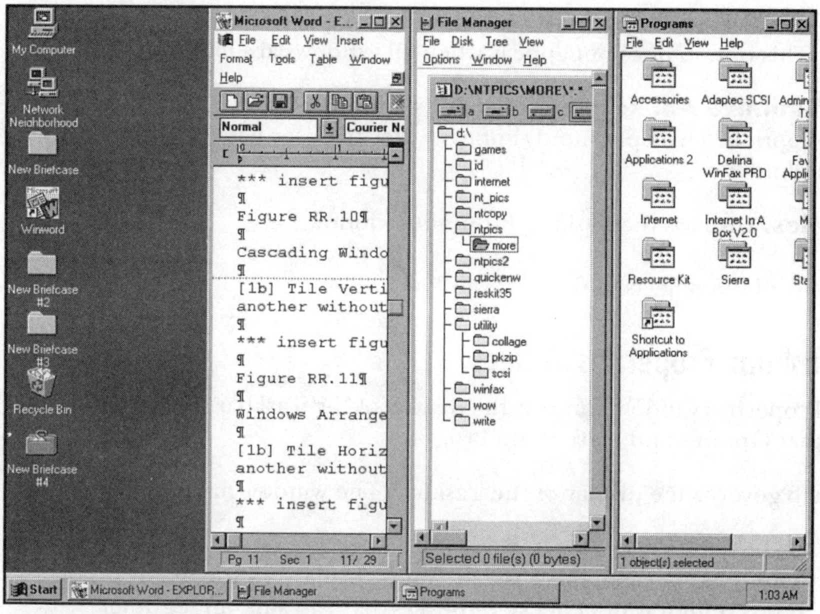

Figure 1.9

Windows arranged vertically.

◆ **Tile Horizontally.** Arranges windows on top of one another without any overlap, as shown in figure 1.10.

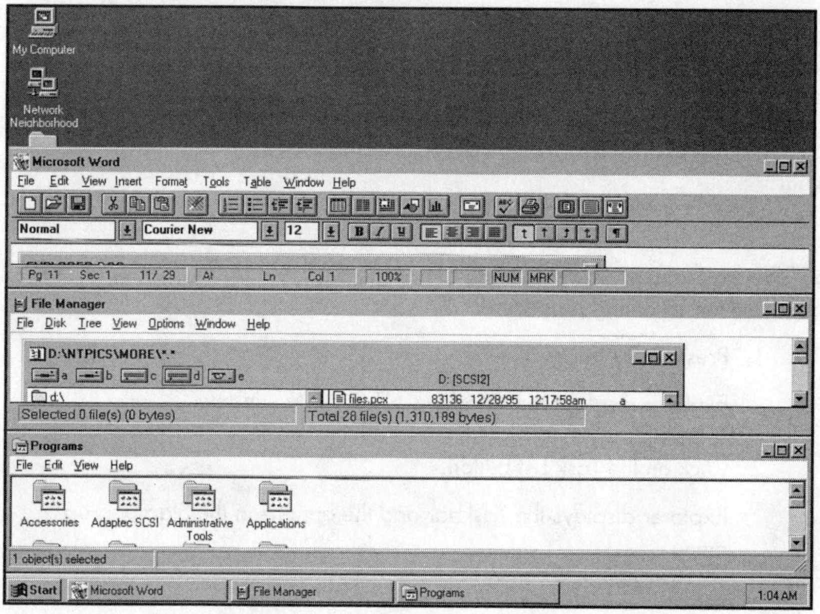

Figure 1.10

Windows arranged horizontally.

- **Minimize All Windows.** Makes all windows disappear from the Root window. This option does not appear when all windows are minimized.
- **Undo Minimize All.** Restores all windows minimized by the Minimize All Windows option. This option only appears after the user has clicked on Minimize All Windows.
- **Properties.** Displays the Taskbar Properties window.

These tools control the objects in the root window.

Using the Taskbar Properties Window

The Taskbar Properties window controls the display of the Taskbar. This window has two tabs: Taskbar Options and Start Menu Programs.

The Taskbar tab governs the display of the Taskbar. The window has four check boxes:

- If Always on top is checked, the Taskbar always displays on top of any other window. If this option is not checked, the Taskbar can sink under other windows.
- If Auto hide is checked, the Taskbar does not display; it does display if the box is unchecked.
- If Show small icons is checked, the size of the icons in the Start pop-up menu is reduced. If the box is unchecked, Explorer uses larger icons in the Start pop-up menu
- If Show clock is checked, Explorer displays a digital clock on the right side of the Taskbar.

Note If you hide the Taskbar, you might later decide to display it again. To display the Taskbar, use the following procedure:

1. Press Ctrl+Alt+Del.

   Explorer displays the Windows NT Security window.

2. Click on the Task List button.

   Explorer displays the Taskbar and the options in the Start pop-up menu.

3. Click on the Settings option in the Start pop-up menu.

   Explorer displays the Taskbar Properties window.

4. Click on the Taskbar icon.

   Explorer displays the Taskbar Properties window.

5. Uncheck the Auto hide check box by clicking on it.

6. Click on the OK button in the Taskbar Properties window.

The Start Menu Programs tab in the Taskbar Properties window enables you to modify the listings displayed by the Programs and Text Document options in the Start pop-up menu.

The top section of the Start Menu Program tab enables you to add or remove the applications and application groups listed by the Programs option in the Start pop-up menu. You can customize the listing most intuitively by using the Add and Remove buttons.

If you plan, however, to add and remove many applications from the Programs listing, it is easier to use the Advanced button. When you click on this button, Explorer displays the Exploring Start Menu window, which closely resembles the File Manager, as you can see in figure 1.11.

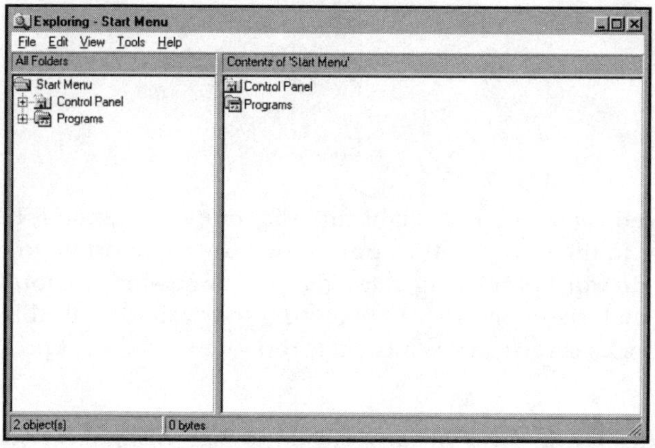

Figure 1.11

The Exploring Start Menu window.

You can use the Delete option in the File menu to remove applications from the Programs listing, or the Explore option in the File menu to add to the Programs listing.

In the bottom half of the Start Menu Programs tab is a section that enables you to remove all of the listings in the Documents option in the Start pop-up menu. All you have to do is click on the Clear button.

Reorienting the Taskbar

By default, the Taskbar appears across the bottom of the screen. If, however, you double-click on the digital clock, the Taskbar displays vertically on the right side of the screen, as shown in figure 1.12.

Figure 1.12
The Taskbar displayed vertically.

Try the Taskbar displayed each way. You might find that one orientation is better than another according to the layout of the applications you use most often. For example, if you mostly do word processing, a longer, narrower window more closely resembles an 8.5-by-11-inch sheet of paper than a wide, short window. In this example, displaying the Taskbar vertically is more appropriate to the word processor's display.

The only drawback to displaying the Taskbar vertically is that the application buttons are dramatically abbreviated. Because the application button includes the application's icon, it is still relatively easy to determine what application the application button represents.

Setting the Digital Clock

When you use the secondary mouse button to click on the digital clock, Explorer displays the Taskbar pop-up menu as shown in figure 1.7, with one exception, an additional menu item appears as the first option in the list: Adjust Date/Time.

When you click on the Adjust Date/Time option, Windows NT Explorer displays the Date/Time window (also accessible through the Control Panel), as shown in figure 1.13.

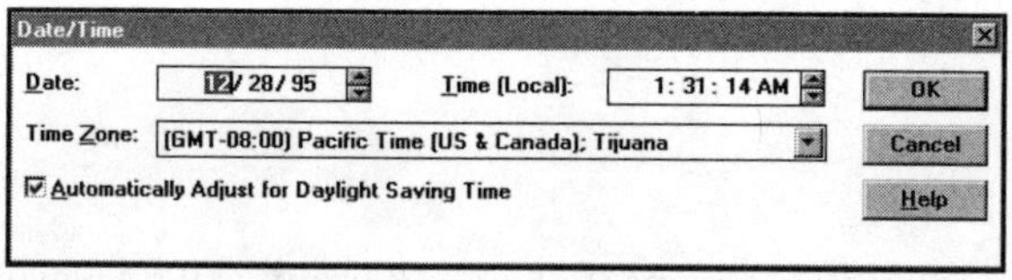

Figure 1.13

The Date/Time window.

You can use this window to set the computer's date and time.

Using the Start Button

On the very left of the Taskbar is the Start button. As its name suggests, Start is almost always the first button you click after you log on.

In case you are totally befuddled by the interface, Microsoft includes an animated message that slides the phrase "<- Start by clicking here" from right to left on the Taskbar if you either take too long to click on the Start button or are a first-time user of Windows NT Explorer.

When you use the primary mouse button to click on the Start button, Windows NT displays the pop-up menu shown in figure 1.14.

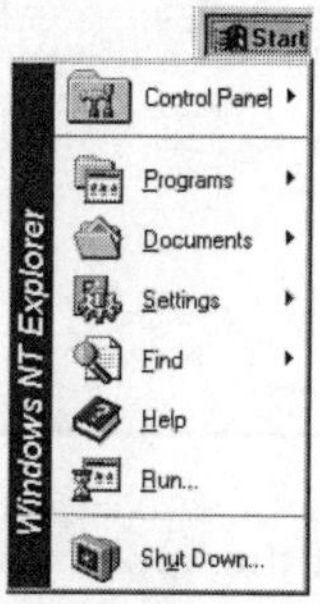

Figure 1.14

The Start pop-up menu.

The options of the Start menu are as follows:

- ◆ Programs
- ◆ Documents
- ◆ Settings
- ◆ Find
- ◆ Help
- ◆ Run
- ◆ Shut Down

An arrow to the right of a menu item means that a child menu will display if you choose the option with the arrow. Child menus can also have arrows beside menu options, in which case, more menus can be displayed at the same time.

The following sections explain each of these options.

Programs Option

Clicking on the Programs option lists all of the application groups that you used to see in Program Manager, as shown in figure 1.15.

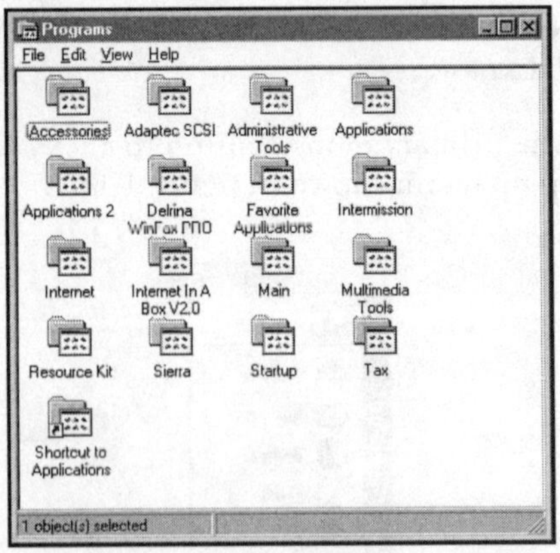

Figure 1.15
The Programs option.

When you move the mouse cursor to one of the application groups, Explorer displays a child menu showing the applications in the application group, as shown in figure 1.22. Clicking on one of the applications in the child menu invokes that application.

Documents Option

Clicking on the Documents option lists documents that you have worked on recently in any application, such as Winword and Framemaker. Clicking on a document name opens the word-processing application and loads the document.

Settings Option

Clicking on the Settings option displays icons for the following:

- Executing the Taskbar application
- Displaying the Control Panel group

If you click on the Taskbar icon, Explorer displays the Taskbar Properties window.

For more information about this window, see the section, "Using the Taskbar Properties Window."

Find Option

Clicking on the Find option enables you to find files, folders, or computers in a network. When you click on Files and folders, Explorer displays the Find: All Files window, as shown in figure 1.16.

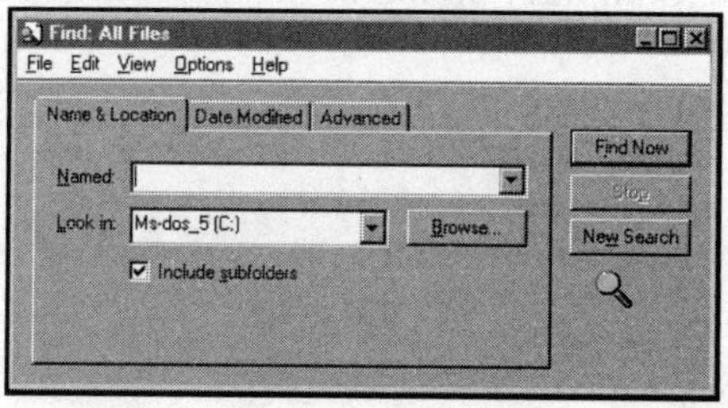

Figure 1.16
The Find: All Files window.

The Find: All Files window has the following three tabs:

- **Name & Location.** Finds files and folders by entering their names, pathnames, or both.
- **Date Modified.** Finds files modified on or between specified dates, as shown in figure 1.17.

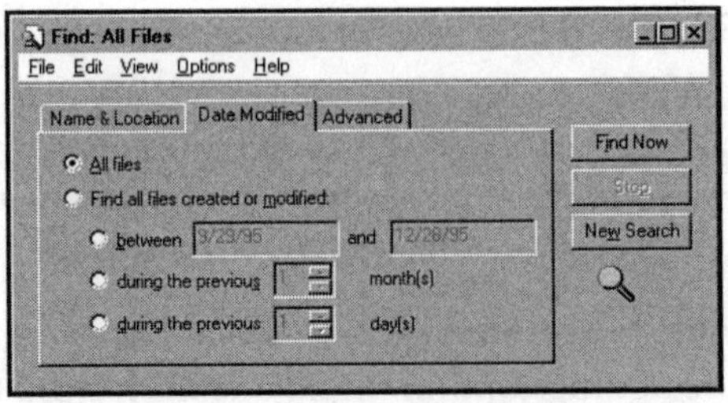

Figure 1.17

The Date Modified tab.

- **Advanced.** Finds files according to type or size, or files containing a specified word or phrase, as shown in figure 1.18.

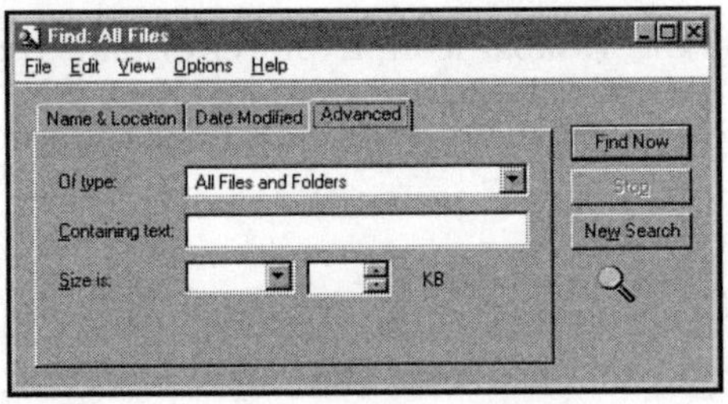

Figure 1.18

The Advanced tab.

You can use the Find option on the Start pop-up menu to find a computer on a network. When you click on the Computer option in the sub menu, Explorer displays the Find: Computer window, as shown in figure 1.19.

Figure 1.19

Finding a computer.

After typing in the name of a computer in the Named: text field, you click on the Find Now button. Explorer reports any name matches of computers on the network.

Help Option

Clicking on the Help option in the Start pop-up menu starts the Help application.

Run Option

Clicking on the Run option in the Start pop-up menu displays the Run window, as shown in figure 1.20.

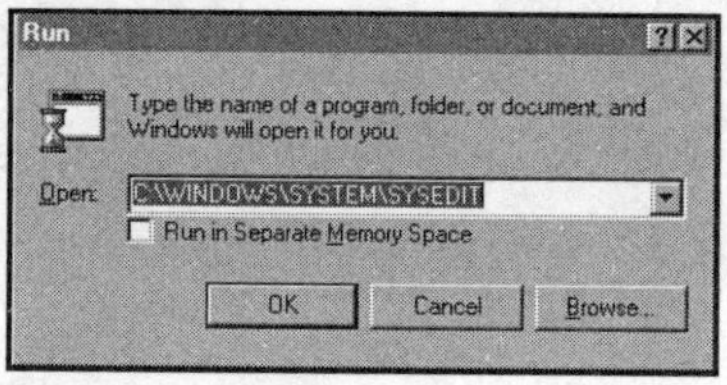

Figure 1.20
The Run window.

In the Open: text field, type the pathname and the name of the application you want to run. This window is the equivalent of the Run option in the File menu of the Program Manager. You use it most often to install new applications on your computer.

Shut Down Option

Clicking on the Shut Down option in the Start pop-up menu displays the Shut Down Windows window.

After clicking on one of the three options, depending on whether you want to restart Windows NT, you click on the Yes button to shut down Windows NT, or the No button to return to Windows NT.

Alternative Uses of the Start Button

The preceding sections used the Start button by clicking it with the primary mouse button. When you click the Start button with the secondary mouse button, Explorer displays a different menu, as shown in figure 1.21.

The following sections explain the functionality of each of the menu options.

Open Option

Clicking on the Open option in the secondary menu displays the Start Menu window with the application group called Programs, as shown in figure 1.22.

Figure 1.21

The secondary menu for the Start button.

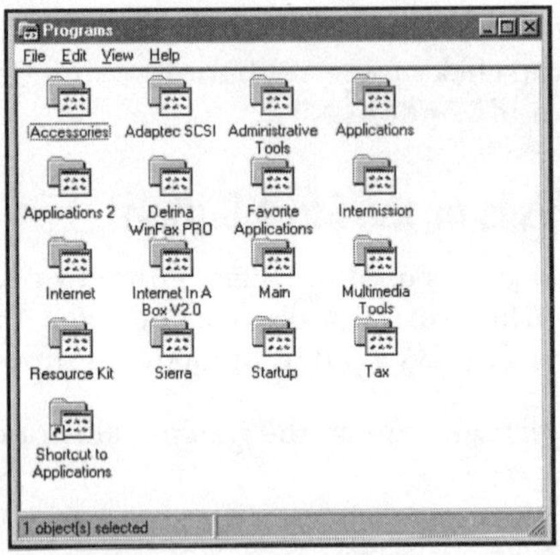

Figure 1.22

The Programs application group.

The programs listed under the secondary Start menu are the same programs that are listed when you click on the Programs option in the Start pop-up menu.

Using the **Open** option in the secondary menu is the easiest to add or delete files or folders from the list of programs displayed by the Programs option. Deleting a file, for example, is as easy as highlighting it and clicking on the Delete option in the File menu.

Explore Option

Clicking on the Explore option in the secondary menu displays the Exploring Start Menu, as shown in figure 1.23.

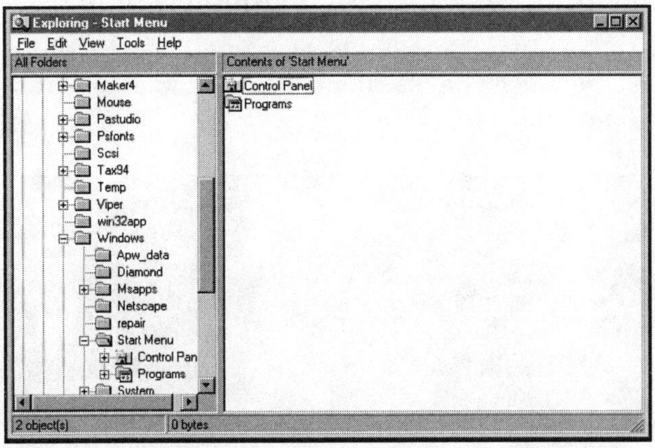

Figure 1.23
The Exploring Start Menu window.

You recognize this display as being similar to the File Manager display. The hierarchy of files and folders is made clear by lines and indentations. The files and folders listed are the same as those listed when you click on the Programs option in the Start pop-up menu.

By clicking on folders, you can reveal or hide their contents.

Find Option

Clicking on the Find Option displays the Find window that enables you to search for files by specifying search criteria.

In the middle of the Taskbar you find buttons for each running application.

Application buttons are valuable because they do not get covered. They work like tabs: clicking on one restores the window or moves the window to the top of the displayed windows.

You might have had the frustrating experience of opening so many applications at the same time that weeding through the windows to find the application you wanted was laborious. It was so easy to lose windows in the heap of running applications.

By listing all running applications, you have instant access to their window by clicking on the button with the application's name. This functionality saves a lot of headaches.

When the running application's window is not minimized, the application button is black-and-white, and appears depressed. When the application's window is minimized, the application button is colored, and appears raised.

Using the Secondary Mouse Button with Application Buttons

When you click on an application button in the Taskbar with the secondary mouse button, Explorer displays a pop-up menu of actions you might want to perform on the application, as shown in figure 1.24.

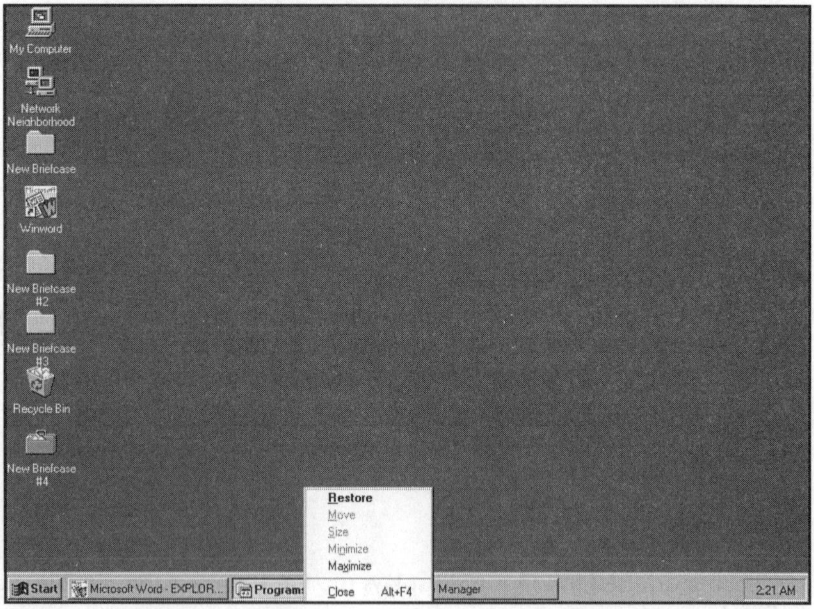

Figure 1.24
The Application button pop-up menu.

You recognize these options from the menu that would display in version 3.*x* if you single-clicked on an icon. The menu options in figure 1.24 have the following functions:

- **Restore.** Displays the window the same size as it was before it was minimized.
- **Move.** Enables you to move a displayed window.
- **Size.** Enables you to change the size of a displayed window.
- **Minimize.** Makes the window disappear.

- **Maximize.** Makes the window as large as the entire screen.
- **Close.** Terminates the application.
- **Run.** Displays the Run window, as shown in figure 1.25, which enables you to display the Clipboard or the Control Panel application group. The Clipboard is a buffer that contains information that you previously copied or cut.

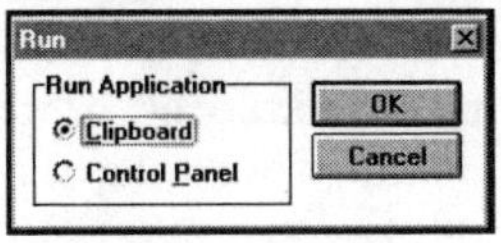

Figure 1.25
The Run window.

Displaying a Minimized Window

You can minimize windows in a variety of ways, including the following:

- Click on the button with a dash in it on the top, right of the Title bar.
- Use the secondary mouse button to click on the application button in the Taskbar. This action displays the Taskbar pop-up menu from which you can click on Mi**n**imize.
- Use the secondary mouse button to click on a blank spot on the Taskbar. This action displays the Taskbar pop-up menu from which you can click on Minimize All Windows.

When you minimize a window, it disappears from the Root window. The application button, however, remains in the Taskbar. To reopen the application, you can perform one of the following tasks:

- Click on the application button in the Taskbar.
- Click on the application button in the Taskbar with the secondary mouse button. When Explorer displays the Application Button pop-up menu, click on the **R**estore option.

Getting rid of icons and replacing them with application buttons on the Taskbar eliminates the problem of trying to find icons burried under layers of windows.

The New Look, Feel, and Functionality of Explorer

If you have worked with Windows 3.*x* or Windows NT 3.*x* in the past, you see that the look, feel, and functionality of the windows in Explorer are different. For example, in the past, when you grabbed the corner of a window and pulled it, only an outline of the window expanded or shrunk. When you released the corner, the window would instantly resize to the shape of the outline. In Explorer, however, when you grab a corner and pull it, the entire window expands or shrinks in real time.

This section examines some of the new features in Windows NT that gives it such a different look and feel from Windows 3.*x* and Windows NT 3.*x*.

Using the Title Bar

The title bar in all Explorer windows is different from that in version 3.*x*. On the upper, left corner of the window in version 3.*x*, you used to see a box with a dash in it, as shown in figure 1.26.

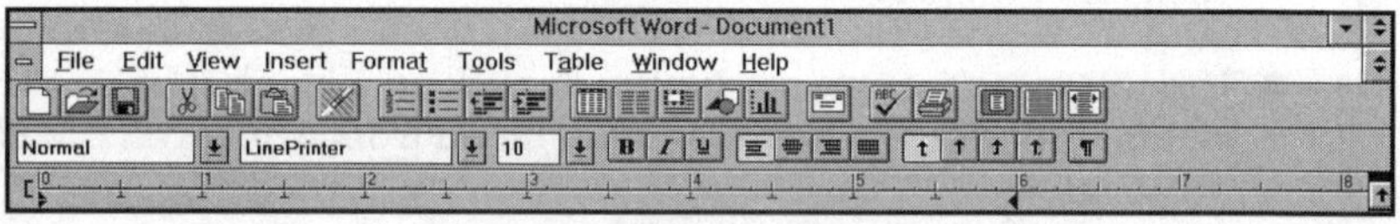

Figure 1.26

The old title bar.

Double-clicking on the dash button terminated the window (and the application running in the window). Single-clicking on the dash button displayed the Control pop-up menu that enabled you to do such things as maximize, minimize, move, raise, lower, and close the window.

In Explorer, the dash button is replaced by a graphic, as shown in figure 1.27.

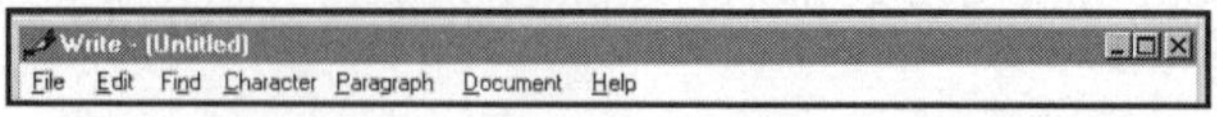

Figure 1.27

The new title bar.

The new icon performs the same function as the dash button—double-clicking on it terminates the window, single-clicking on it reveals the Control menu.

In version 3.*x*, on the right side of the title bar are the maximize and minimize buttons represented by buttons containing an up and down arrow, respectively (refer to fig. 1.26).

These buttons are replaced by three new buttons (refer to fig. 1.27). The functions of the buttons are as follows:

- The button with a dash minimizes the window.
- The button with a square maximizes the window, meaning that the window expands to the size of the screen.
- The button with an "X" terminates the window.

The "X" button provides a way to terminate a window using a single click. (The icon on the extreme left side of the Title bar requires that you double-click on it to terminate a window.)

Using the Help System

On some windows you see a button with a question mark in it on the right side of the Title bar. This button enables you to access pop-up help windows. If, for example, you click on the question mark with the primary mouse button, the mouse cursor changes to a question mark. If you then click on an object in the window, a brief description of the object you clicked on pops up, as shown in figure 1.28.

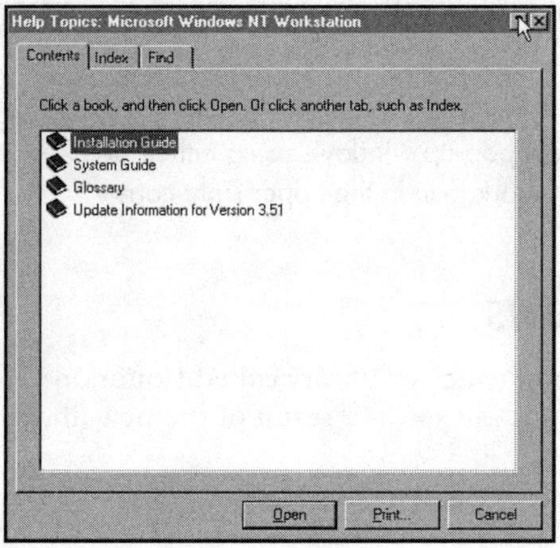

Figure 1.28
Using the question mark button.

If you click on a window object, such as a text entry field, with the secondary mouse button, the What's This? pop-up window displays, as shown in figure 1.29.

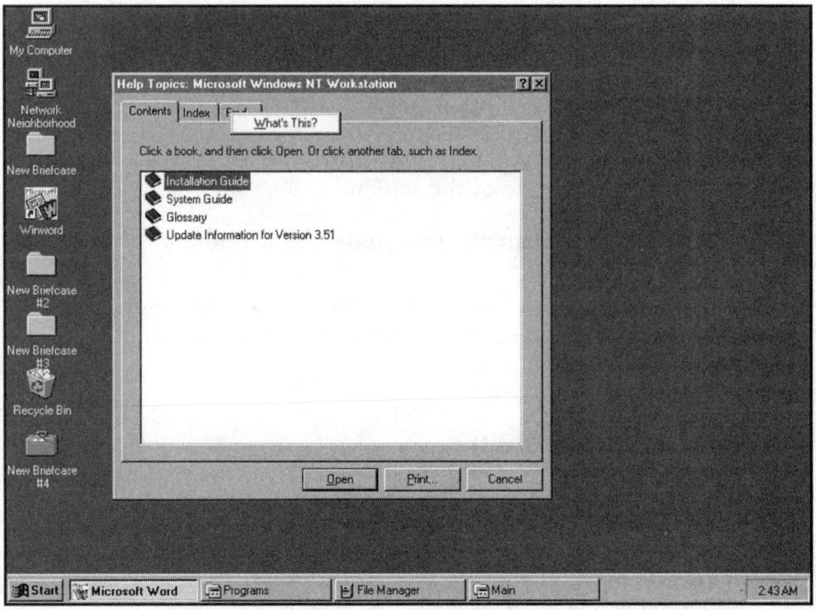

Figure 1.29
The What's This pop-up option.

If you click on the What's This window with the primary mouse button, Windows NT displays brief, context-sensitive help.

Note You can only access help pop-up windows using either mouse button when the window has a question mark icon in the upper right corner.

Using Tabs in Windows

Windows NT Explorer uses a new windows library called Common Controls. One of the additions to windows that you will see as a result of the new library is the use of tabs.

Tabs function just like tabs on a manila folder: they stick out so you can find folders easily.

When you layer window upon window, it is easy to lose windows under the pile. The advantage of using tabs is that the tab for each pane on the window is always visible. Whenever you click on a tab, its pane moves to the top.

Note In the latest version of Windows NT Workstation, you can raise a window to the top of the stack of windows by clicking anywhere on the window that you want to raise. This feature alone is worth the cost of the upgrade!

Tabs can run across the top of a window as well as down the sides.

Using Folders

The visual metaphor of a folder suggests that the Explorer folder, just like a manila folder, can hold files and other folders. The use of folders is not entirely new to Windows. File Manager in version 3.*x* uses a folder icon as a symbol for a directory. When you click on a folder in File Manager, it actually appears to open and its contents are then displayed in the right side of File Manager. File Manager uses the visual metaphor of a hierarchy to suggest the relationship between directories and files.

Windows NT Explorer disassociates the folder icon with directories and hierarchies. Whenever you choose the Open option in any of the Windows NT Explorer menus, the contents of folders, briefcases, and the Recycle Bin display, as shown in figure 1.30.

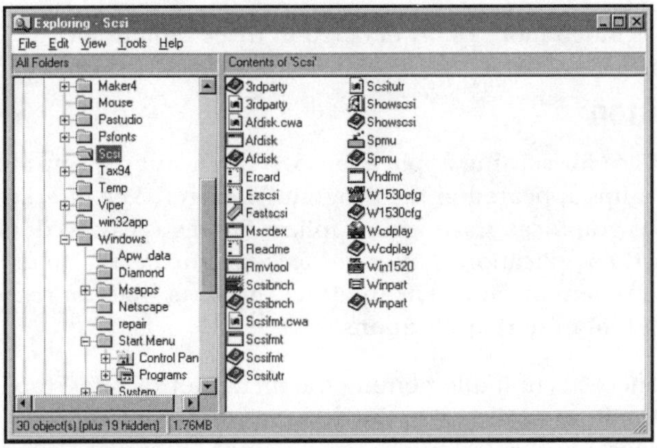

Figure 1.30

Using folders in Windows NT.

Note You can change the display in figure 1.30 to a hierarchically oriented display by choosing Details in the View menu. When Large Icon or Small Icon is selected, the display uses the icons of paper and folders.

Instead of seeing the folder in figure 1.30 as representing a directory, you just see the folder as something unto itself. For this reason, the use of the folder in Explorer is based more on what a folder in the real world is instead of a computer organizational concept: a directory. In this way, Windows NT Explorer provides a more intuitive interface made of images of commonplace things.

When you double-click on a folder, it opens to reveal its contents, which might be files or other folders.

Examining the New Look of Windows

Not only have the icons in windows changed, but the look of the windows has also changed. For example, when you pull down menus, you see a three-dimensional menu instead of the two-dimensional rendering found in version 3.*x*. Dividers that separate menu items in 3.*x* menus are simple lines, but in Explorer, dividers are carefully shadowed, three-dimensional crevices.

Note If you have worked on X systems with GUIs such as Motif or Solaris, you will notice similar images in Windows NT Explorer. The menus, for example, look the same. The use of horizontal scrolling in file listings and the use of folders to hold files is also reminiscent of Solaris.

Everything in Explorer is much more richly detailed in three dimensions.

Examining the Desktop

In version 3.*x*, the interface for starting applications was application groups filled with icons. All application groups appeared in the Program Manager. The interface was easy to use because it was graphical; starting an application was as easy as double-clicking on the icon for the application. This interface was much easier to use than entering commands at a system prompt. The interface, however, did not represent anything; it was simply a tool to start applications.

Windows NT Explorer succeeds in implementing the metaphor of a desktop. The desktop in Explorer is the Root window. On the desktop you can place many things, not just application groups. On the desktop you can place, for example, a file, an application group, a printer icon, an application icon, a folder; any icon that you find in any folder can be placed on the Root window for direct access, just as you might set out all of the items you need to do your work on a real desktop.

For people who have used GUIs such as Motif, Solaris, or System 7 by Apple, the desktop metaphor is not new. For those who have used only Windows 3.*x* or Windows

NT 3.*x*, the desktop metaphor is a welcome surprise. It frees applications from the confines of application groups and the trouble of memorizing what applications reside in which application groups.

Application Groups in Explorer

Application groups have not entirely disappeared. You can still create collections of applications because you tend to use them in conjunction with one another. If you bring forward the settings in your CONFIG.SYS and AUTOEXEC.BAT files when you install Windows NT, you can still access those application groups by choosing Programs in the Start pop-up menu.

Summary

The latest version of Windows NT not only offers added functionality, but a dramatically redesigned user interface. The interface resembles Unix interfaces, most notably Solaris and Motif. Users can use the Root window, called the desktop, to display icons for files, devices, folders, briefcases, and other programming objects. The freedom to place an icon representing hardware or software on the desktop enables easy access to all of these elements. Gone is the Program Manager that served as the root window for application groups. Application groups still exist, but they do not form the centerpiece for application activation.

Windows NT Explorer supports the new library, Common Controls. This library enables new window widgets, such as horizontal and vertical tabs within windows. Both tabs and the Taskbar help users locate specific windows when windows are piled upon windows.

The Explorer interface is so dramatically different from the 3.*x* interface that the new user might first experience shock. The success with which Microsoft engineers have designed a more intuitive interface using the desktop as the central metaphor enables even new users to quickly master the Explorer interface.

The Explorer interface made only the Program Manager obsolete. All of the other familiar applications and application groups, such as the Control Panel, found in version 3.*x* remain in Explorer. Because of the new freedom found in the desktop, however, the emphasis shifts away from application groups and toward a customized desktop.

CHAPTER 2

Mastering the Windows NT Application Groups

In Chapter 1, you learned the basics of the way Windows NT works. You also became familiar with the Windows Explorer and the basic skills you need to know to manipulate windows. This chapter introduces you to the members of Windows NT application groups and the following topics:

- Getting to know the desktop
- Introducing the application groups
- Running multiple applications

Getting to Know the Desktop

After you launch Windows NT and successfully log on, you are presented with the desktop. System commands are represented by pictures on the Windows NT desktop. These pictures take the form of icons, buttons, controls, and parts of application and document windows. You communicate by acting on one of these pictures, clicking a mouse button, or pressing a key.

Tip In MS-DOS and Unix, you often use command-line switches to define the action the command is to take. Windows NT assigns the same information for a command by using option buttons, check boxes, list boxes, and combination boxes in a dialog box.

When Windows NT requires information about command options, a dialog box containing various controls appears. Dialog boxes are Windows NT's pictorial way of representing familiar command-line options. A key difference between working at a command prompt and working on the Windows NT desktop is that you do not have to remember the exact command switches—you just have to specify the options you want in the dialog box.

Tip In Windows NT, you also can run a command-prompt session by double-clicking on the Command Prompt icon in the Main menu. The set of commands available is similar to that in MS-DOS.

If you are familiar with character-based environments, you might find working on the desktop awkward at first. After you understand the parts and get used to the rhythm, however, you probably will find the desktop more comfortable than the command lines of other operating systems.

Parts of the Desktop

The Windows NT desktop is organized into three layers: the Root window, the wallpaper layer, and the application layer. As figure 2.1 shows, each layer has particular functions attached to it.

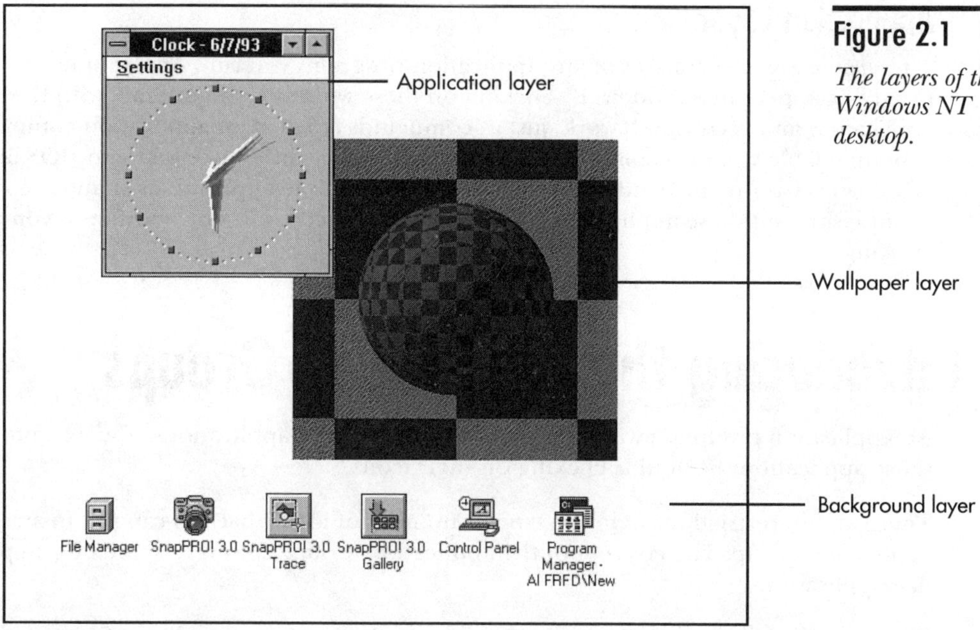

Figure 2.1
The layers of the Windows NT desktop.

The Root Window

The Root window is the background upon which everything else is laid. Uncovered, it appears as a blue background. You can place icons on the Root window that represent files, folders, applications, and devices. Windows NT 3.*x* did not have a Root window. You could only place icons within application group windows. (When you minimized applications in NT 3.*x*, an icon appeared on the Wallpaper, but its placement there was temporary: when you terminated the application, the icon disappeared.)

The Root window in Explorer also has functionality. When you right-click on it, a pop-up menu displays. The menu options are explained in Chapter 4.

Wallpaper Layer

The *wallpaper layer*, also called the Root window, consists of a picture that fills the screen. Its purpose is to provide an individualized viewing screen so that you find working at your PC more comfortable.

Note Technically, wallpaper is a bit map that is displayed onscreen and stored in your Windows NT directory in a file with a BMP extension.

Application Layer

The *application layer* consists of any application programs you run. Application programs appear in a window. By clicking on these windows, you interact with the application and accomplish work, just as commands typed at an application command prompt enable you to accomplish the same work. A key difference between DOS and Windows NT is that in Windows NT, you can run multiple applications simultaneously (multitask), and these applications communicate directly with one another as you are working.

Introducing the Application Groups

An application group is a window that holds the icons of applications. You execute those applications by double-clicking on their icons.

There are no restrictions as to the type or number of icons that you can put in an application group. The concept of the application group, however, is one of grouping like applications.

When you work at your desk, you have certain tasks that you typically perform as part of your job. You also have tools with which you perform these tasks.

Windows NT application groups enable you to organize the applications you use into a window that represents that task. If you want to work on a sales report, for instance, double-click on the sales report group icon. The application group window that opens contains all the programs you need for that task. You might have your spreadsheet, calculator, word processor, notepad, and network mail programs grouped together, for example. To access the tool you need at the moment, double-click on the program-item icon.

When you install applications, they create their own application group. It might contain a game icon with icons for other games that you can preview (made by the same company).

Application Groups were the main organizational feature of Windows NT 3.*x*. In Explorer, however, they are buried. You can display application groups by right-clicking on the Start button and selecting Open. When you click on the Programs icon, all of the application groups you used in NT 3.*x* display, as long as you chose to carry the application groups over into NT when you installed it.

Vestiges of application groups are also apparent in the lists displayed with the Start button. Left-clicking on the Start button displays the names of the application groups you used in NT 3.*x*. When you highlight one of the list items, a child menu appears showing the applications in the application group.

Engineers chose to replace application groups with application lists in Explorer because the lists make the applications more accessible. Changing the content of the application groups and changing the properties of the list items, however, are more difficult when using the lists alone. To change the content of an application group or to change the property of an item on a list, it is easier to use the application groups themselves.

Tip

Use a reasonable number of application groups on your Windows NT desktop. Create groups that represent the major tasks you perform. Keep in mind that creating large numbers of application groups takes resources away from working applications. Later in this chapter you are shown the way to add items to application groups.

Several application groups can contain the same program-item icon, which enables you to create groups that represent the tasks you commonly perform at your PC (and have as many groups as you want). Your writing group, for example, might contain your word processor, style checker, dictionary, thesaurus, and encyclopedia programs. Your leisure group might contain various game programs, as well as the same word processor and encyclopedia. As you change tasks, you open the application group representing that task. All your tools are at hand and ready to go.

Windows NT creates six application groups when you install it: Main, Accessories, Games, StartUp, Administrative Tools, and Applications. These groups are explained in the following sections.

The Main Group

Just as you have tools you use to organize the way you work (such as a desktop calendar or a to-do list), Windows NT includes application tools you can use to organize its environment. These tools are in the *Main* application group, as shown in figure 2.2.

Figure 2.2
The Main group.

You find the following applications in the Main group:

- **File Manager.** Enables you to perform many file and disk operations, including running applications, formatting disks, managing file directories, and so on.
- **Mail.** Enables you to send and receive mail across your network.
- **Schedule+.** Enables you to maintain a calendar for yourself and to schedule meetings by accessing the calendars of other people on your network.
- **Control Panel.** Enables you to set up many Windows features by using various utilities provided by Windows NT.
- **Print Manager.** Enables you to manage Windows NT's print spooler. You can begin and stop print jobs, and change print job priorities here.
- **ClipBook Viewer.** Serves as a "transfer agent" to move data from one Windows NT application to another, including programs running on different networked computers.
- **Command Prompt.** Enables you to open a command-line window to perform operations.

  The Control menu on the Command Prompt window has a new option, Properties. You display the Control menu by clicking on the dash button in the upper left corner of the window. The Properties option enables you to adjust the cursor size, command history size, fonts, screen size and position, and screen colors. The Command Prompt Properties window operates identically to the Console Windows Properties window. For more information about changing any of the window properties, refer to the discussion of the Command Prompt Properties window in Chapter 4, "Learning How to Perform Basic Tasks with Windows NT."

- **Windows NT Setup.** Enables you to modify some of the basic Windows NT operational parameters. You can, for instance, change video-display resolutions by using the Setup program.
- **PIF Editor.** Enables you to establish special settings so that DOS applications run correctly under Windows NT. These settings are established in a program information file (PIF).
- **Windows NT Help.** Provides help on all aspects of using Windows NT.
- **Introducing Windows NT.** Presents a tutorial on using Windows NT and its features.

The Accessories Group

The *Accessories* application group is shown in figure 2.3.

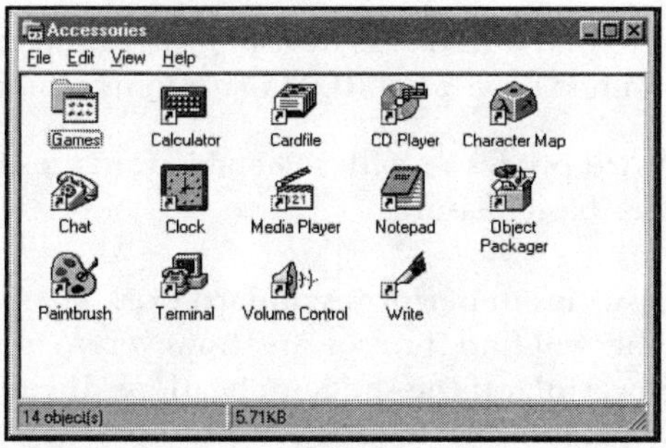

Figure 2.3
The Accessories group.

You find the following accessory application programs in the Accessories group:

- **Calculator.** Provides an on-screen calculator for math operations.
- **Cardfile.** Provides the same functionality as a desktop card file.
- **Clock.** Displays the time in either analog or digital form.
- **Notepad.** Provides a quick, easy-to-use ASCII editor for composing short notes or editing small ASCII files.
- **Paintbrush.** Provides a basic drawing package that enables you to produce graphics suitable for inclusion in documents produced by Windows NT applications. Supports PCX, BMP, and MSP formats.
- **Chat.** Enables you to conduct a "live" conversation with another user of your network.

- **Terminal.** Provides basic terminal-emulation capabilities and enables you to access other computers by modem or serial-port connection.
- **3270 Emulator.** Emulates an IBM 3270 terminal for users who need to access data on mainframes that expect this type of terminal.
- **Character Map.** Enables you to insert characters not found on most keyboards, such as extended characters and special characters provided in symbol fonts.
- **Sound Recorder.** Enables you to record sounds that are input through a microphone attached to your sound board.
- **Volume Control.** Enables you to adjust the volume of the channels on your sound card.
- **Media Player.** Provides access to playback capabilities for any multimedia device or service, from sound files to Video for Windows files.
- **CD Player.** Enables you to play audio CDs by using the sound services of your computer. Of course, you must have a CD-ROM drive to use this applet.
- **Write.** Provides a basic word processor with selectable fonts, a search-and-replace function, and other basic features.

You can use the preceding accessories to perform standard work tasks as soon as you install Windows NT. You probably will find it necessary, however, to augment these basic applications with more powerful, off-the-shelf applications. If you plan on doing extensive word processing, for example, Write probably will not suit your needs. Instead, a word processor with more features than Write provides (such as Word for Windows, WordPerfect for Windows, or Ami Pro) is required.

Administrative Tools

The *Administrative Tools* group contains tools that enable you to perform system-level tasks on your computer, such as adding users, configuring hard drives, backing up the system, and monitoring security.

Note As an individual user, you probably do not use these tools; Windows NT grants the privilege of using most of the features to the system administrator.

The Administrative Tools group is shown in figure 2.4.

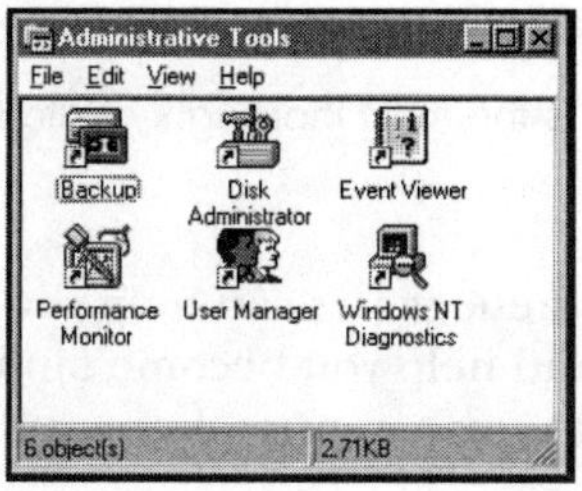

Figure 2.4
The Administrative Tools group.

You find the following programs in the Administrative Tools group:

- **User Manager.** Enables you to add user logon accounts to the system and to grant user privileges.
- **Disk Administrator.** Enables you to configure hard drives, set up partitions, assign drive letters, and create fault-tolerant disk mirroring.
- **Performance Monitor.** Enables you to represent the speed performance of each segment of the system and operating system graphically so that you can troubleshoot potential performance problems.
- **Backup.** Enables you to back up data to a tape drive.
- **Event Viewer.** Provides a view of the event log, which lists everything that happens on the system. This application enables you to review potential security problems or system problems by examining relevant actions taken by the operating system.

Games

The *Games* application group (as shown in figure 2.5) contains the following three games: Solitaire, Minesweeper, and Freecell.

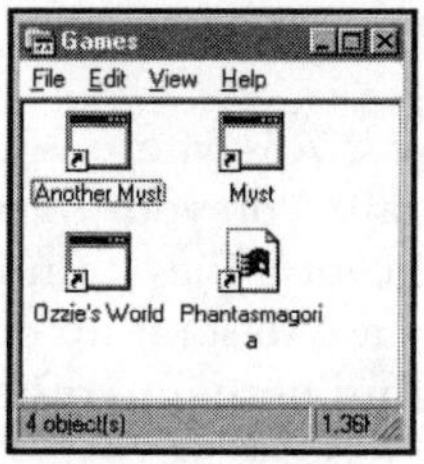

Figure 2.5
The Games application group.

Note Microsoft notes that Solitaire is the most thoroughly tested program they ever produced!

Besides their recreational function, these games can help you practice basic Windows NT skills, such as using the mouse, and help you become familiar with Windows NT buttons, boxes, and scroll bars so that you can use other applications more effectively.

The Startup Group

The *Startup* application group is where Windows NT places applications that begin automatically. As figure 2.6 illustrates, Windows NT does not automatically install any programs in this group. Add to this group any applications that you want to run automatically whenever Windows NT starts up. The Startup group, therefore, serves much like the DOS AUTOEXEC.BAT file.

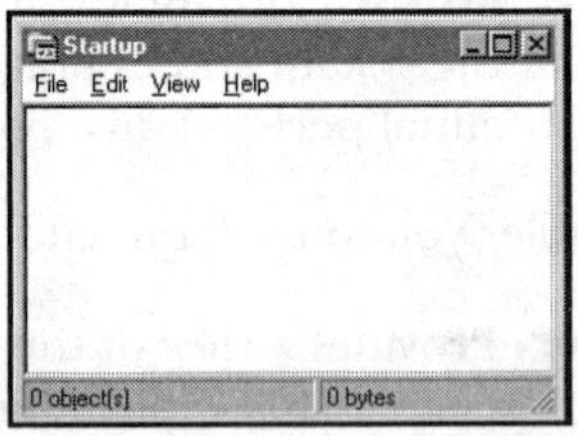

Figure 2.6
The Startup group.

File Manager is a good application to add to the Startup group, especially if you use it often. Loaded automatically, File Manager analyzes your hard drive's directory structure during startup. The next time you access File Manager after startup, File Manager does not have to repeat this analysis. If you start File Manager from its application group each time you need it, you have to wait while File Manager analyzes your drive's directory structure every time.

The Applications Group

The *Applications* group, as shown in figure 2.7, is where Windows NT places all of the application programs it finds already installed on your hard disk. Windows NT searches your drives and sets up the application files it finds in this group. If Windows NT misses one of your applications, you have to set it up on your own. You probably want to reorganize the applications you find here into other groups that more accurately reflect your working tasks.

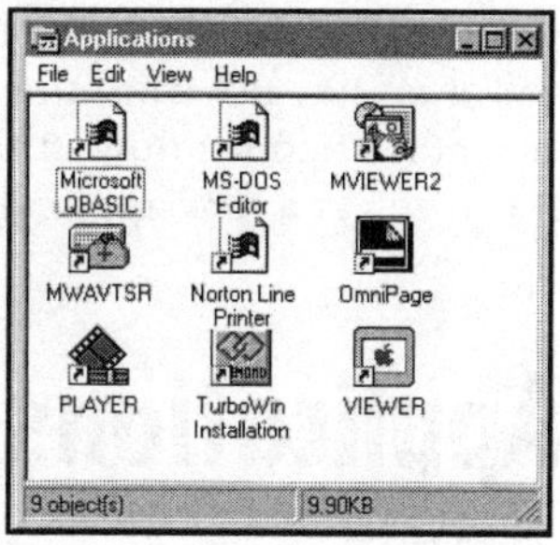

Figure 2.7
The Applications group.

Modifying an Application Group

When you open an application group, the application group window appears in the same position it held the last time it was opened. If this position is not convenient, several methods for moving and resizing the window are available.

If you want to move the window, point to its title bar with the mouse pointer, press the mouse button, and drag the window anywhere in the Program Manager's workspace. After the window is in position, release the mouse button.

If you want to change the application group's window size, point at one of its borders with the mouse pointer. After the pointer changes to a double arrow, press the mouse button down, and drag the border to increase or decrease the window's size. You see an outline representation of the new size as you drag. After the window is the size you want, release the mouse button.

If you want to arrange several open application-group windows to get better access to the contents, use the <u>T</u>ile or <u>C</u>ascade options on the <u>W</u>indow menu (see fig. 2.8).

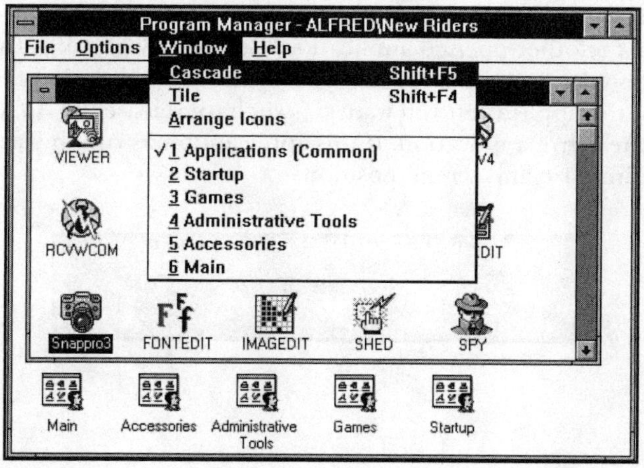

Figure 2.8
The Window menu.

The Tile option arranges the open windows edge to edge, like tiles on a wall. The Cascade option arranges the windows so that they fall from the upper left corner of the workspace toward the lower right corner. Each window's title bar and Control menu box are visible so that you easily can select a new application-group window.

Running Multiple Applications

One of the principal advantages of a windowed environment is its capability to run several applications at once. Windows NT makes it easy to switch between applications and also to find out which applications are running.

Tip

The method of multitasking used by Windows NT and Windows 95 provides an advantage over Windows 3.1. Windows NT and Windows 95 give each program its own slice of time, shifting the timeslice around all the programs so they all have a fair chance to execute. As a result, while one program works, so do all other programs.

In Windows 3.1, however, each program has to wait for the others to voluntarily yield the computer's resources before it can run. One busy application can prevent all applications from accomplishing work.

The easiest way to switch among applications is to click anywhere on the application window of the application you want to activate. The application's title bar is highlighted, and the application window moves to the top of the stack of running windows. The application is ready for input and commands.

You also can use the Alt+Tab key combination to switch between windows. While pressing this key combination, a box appears in the center of your screen (see fig. 2.9), listing the name of another opened application. Repeatedly pressing Tab while holding down Alt cycles you through the names of all running applications. When you reach the name of the application you want to switch to, release the Alt key. That application becomes the active application. If this application was running as an icon, it is restored to its original size and screen position.

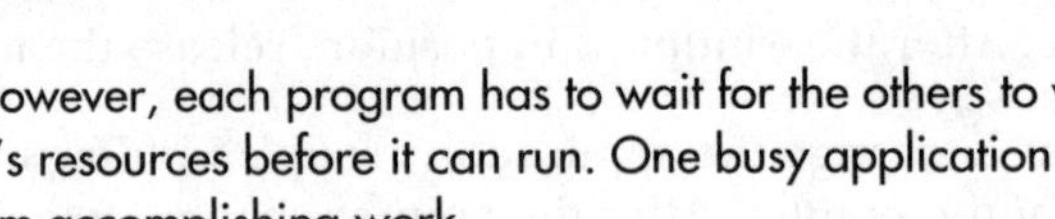

Figure 2.9

Switching among applications by pressing Alt+Tab.

The second option is Alt+Esc. This option works like Alt+Tab, except that no dialog box appears. You move among the applications on the desktop. Each press of the key combination (Esc, while you hold down Alt) activates the next application on the list of running tasks. The application window or application icon is highlighted. Its open or minimized status does not change when the new task is made active, however. Icons become active, but they are not restored.

Summary

This chapter introduced you to the key parts of the Windows NT desktop, including the background, the wallpaper, and the application layer. The functions associated with each also were identified.

This chapter also explained the way Windows NT provides a powerful substitute for the command-line prompt. The concept of building application groups that represent your working style suggests that you can be more productive in Windows NT than at the operating-system prompt.

You learned that you can arrange the applications that help you accomplish your work the way you want on your desktop. Procedures for running and exiting applications also show that Windows NT can provide great flexibility as you work.

CHAPTER 3

Using Windows NT Applets

The usefulness of Windows NT lies in its 32-bit architecture and 32-bit commercial applications that are designed to run on the Windows NT platform. There are also some useful, albeit relatively simple, applications that come with Windows NT. These applications—which typically are scaled-down versions of more sophisticated, off-the-shelf applications—are commonly referred to as applets.

This chapter looks at Windows NT applets, and discusses the following:

- Surveying single-user applets
- Exploring multiuser applets
- Using administrative tools

Once you master Windows NT applets, you will have mastered much of the functionality the operating system has to offer.

Surveying Single-User Applets

There are several single-user applets included with Windows NT. Most of these are identical to their Windows 95 counterparts; some are enhanced versions of the Windows 95 applets; some are different. These Windows applets are described in the following sections.

- **3270 Emulator.** The 3270 Emulator is a basic terminal-emulation program that enables connection to an IBM 3270 mainframe. Emulating an IBM 3178/79 terminal, this applet enables you to connect to the host computer in one of the following three environments: Virtual Machine/Conversation Monitor System (VM/CMS), Time Sharing Options (TSO), and Customer Information Control Systems (CICS). The 3270 Emulator is shown in figure 3.1.

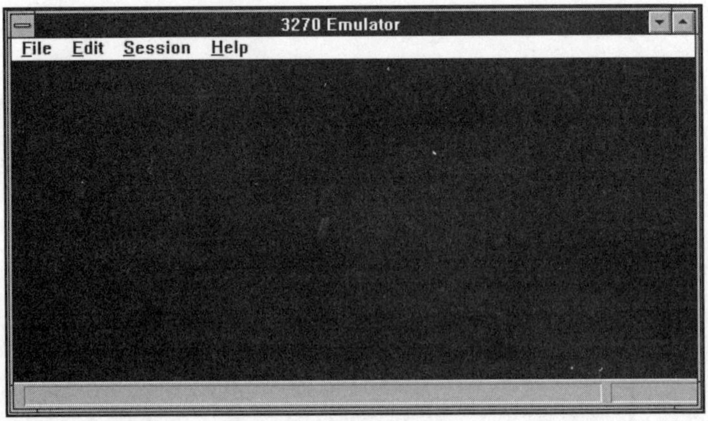

Figure 3.1
The 3270 Emulator adds built-in communications power to Windows NT.

- **Calculator.** Calculator provides the basic functions of a normal hand-held calculator. You can optionally change its display to that of a scientific calculator to provide additional capabilities.

- **Cardfile.** Cardfile features a simple flat-file database that stores addresses and other commonly accessed information. Because it has no querying capability, its usefulness is primarily for small amounts of data.

- **CD Player.** The Windows NT CD Player enables you to play audio CDs on your CD-ROM drive. CD Player is shown in figure 3.2.

- **Character Map.** Character Map contains a grid that displays the entire character set for a specific font. This applet is useful when you need to use a special "high-ANSI" character, and do not know the Alt+num keyboard equivalent. Use Character Map to copy special characters to the Clipboard and paste them into other Windows applications.

Figure 3.2

The CD Player.

- **Clock.** Displays an on-screen digital or analog clock showing your PC's system time.

- **File Manager.** Enhanced in Windows NT, File Manager is used to perform file-management tasks within Windows NT. File Manager eliminates the need to perform command-line operations on such activities as creating and deleting directories, moving and copying files, and running EXE files. File Manager is shown in figure 3.3.

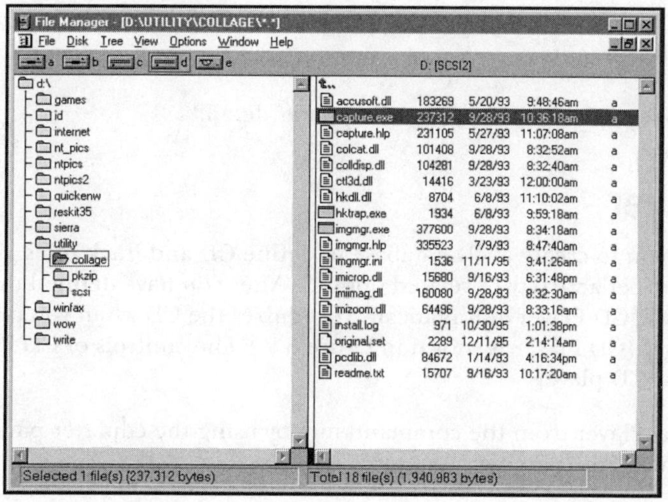

Figure 3.3

The File Manager.

- **Media Player.** Media Player is used to play multimedia files, such as WAV and MIDI sound files, and AVI (Video for Windows) video clips. It also can be used with any Media Control Interface (MCI) connected to your PC.

- **Notepad.** Notepad is a basic text editor for working with ANSI text files. It provides limited editing features, similar to DOS's EDIT utility.

- **Paintbrush.** Paintbrush is a useful paint program for working with BMP or PCX graphics. Although its tool palette and features are much more limited than commercial paint applications, Paintbrush is very useful for basic bit-map manipulation.

- **PIF Editor.** PIF Editor is a special utility that creates and edits program information files (PIFs).

Note Program information files (PIFs) are used by Windows NT to run character-based DOS applications.

- **Sound Recorder.** Sound Recorder is like an on-screen audio tape recorder. It enables you to record, play, and even edit WAV sound files. You can also use the Sound Recorder to change the format of saved sound files. To change the format of a sound file, see the section "Converting Sound Formats in Sound Recorder" later in this chapter.

- **Terminal.** Terminal is a basic communications program that enables you to connect to remote computers, online services (such as CompuServe), bulletin-board services, and mainframes. This applet provides TTY, DEC VT-100, and DEC VT-52 terminal-emulation support.

- **Write.** Write is a basic word-processing program you can use to write letters and view WRI documents.

The following sections explain these applets in greater detail.

Using CD Player

This applet enables you to create a CD database to define CD and track titles, define the order of play, and set a variety of related options. After you have defined the title and/or tracks of a CD, CD Player automatically recognizes the CD when you place it in the CD-ROM drive. (CD Player is shown in figure 3.2.) The controls of CD Player mimic those of a real CD player.

You can also start CD Player from the command line by using the cdplayer parameters, /play and /track. For example:

```
> cdplayer /play [drive][trackName]
> cdplayer /play [/track | trackList]
```

Here, drive is the name of the CD-ROM drive—for example, d:. trackName must include the drive name with the name of the track—for example, e:\track04.cda (the .cda extension is required). If you want to play the playlist on drive d:, use the backslash, as follows:

```
> cd player /play d:\
```

The /track parameter plays the tracks in the specified track list. The track list is a list of tracks to play. The track list overrides any track list embedded in the CD. The /play parameter must precede the /track parameter.

The trackList parameter can be used with the /track parameter to specify the track list. The track list is the list of tracknames to play. Tracknames are preceded by the CD-ROM drive letter.

To play track04, for example, you would type the following command:

```
> cdplayer /play d:\track04.cda
```

To play three different tracks, you would type the following command:

```
> cdplayer /play /track d:\track06.cda d:\track02.cda d:\track04.cda
```

Now that you know how to play sound media, the next applet explains how to play other kinds of media.

Using the Media Player

The interface for the Media Player resembles a tape recorder, as shown in figure 3.4.

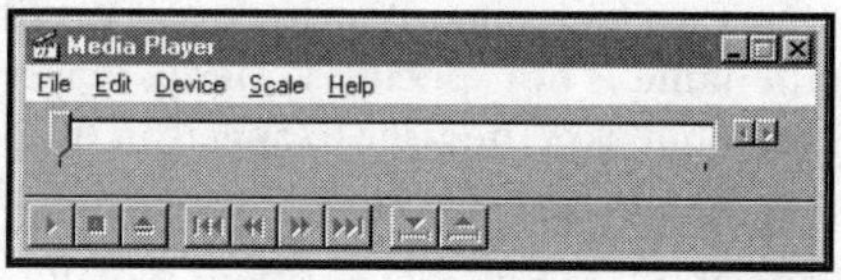

Figure 3.4
The Media Player.

The Device menu enables you to specify the kind of media to play. The media can be any of the following:

- Video for Windows
- Sound files
- MIDI sequencer files
- CD audio

The buttons on Media Player enable you to play, stop, fast forward, rewind, and pause the playing media.

To run Media Player from the command line, use the following command:

```
> mplay32 [parameter] [fileName]
```

fileName is the name of the file or device Media Player plays. Table 3.1 lists the parameters you can use with the mplay32 command.

Table 3.1
mplay32 Parameters

Parameter	Description
/close	Closes a file after it has been played. You can use this parameter only after using the /play parameter.
/embedding	Runs an OLE server.
/midi [fileName]	Opens a MIDI file. If the filename is not specified, Media Player opens a dialog box that asks the user to specify a file.
/open [fileName]	Opens the specified file. If the filename is not specified, Media Player opens a dialog box that asks the user to specify a file.
/play [fileName]	Plays the specified file. If the filename is not specified, Media Player opens a dialog box that asks the user to specify a file.
/vfw [fileName]	Opens a Video for Windows (.VFW) file. If the filename is not specified, Media Player opens a dialog box that asks the user to specify a file.
/wave [fileName]	Opens a wave (.WAV) file. If the filename is not specified, Media Player opens a dialog box that asks the user to specify a file.

Use these parameters to affect the playing of the media.

Converting Sound Formats in Sound Recorder

You can use the Sound Recorder to change the format of saved sound files. To convert a sound file, use the following procedure:

1. In the Sound Recorder window, click on the Properties option in the File menu.

   Windows NT displays the Properties For Sound window.

2. Click on the down arrow in the Choose from box and click on All formats, Playback formats, or Recording formats.

3. Click on the Convert Now button.

   Windows NT displays the Sound Selection window.

4. Use the down arrows in the Name, Format, and Attributes boxes to specify the attributes of the sound format you want to save the sound file as.

5. Click on the OK button. This action confirms the format selection.

6. Click on the OK button in the Properties for Sound window. The Properties for Sound window disappears.

Once you change the sound format, it is just as easy to change it back to its original format using the same procedure.

Exploring Multiuser Applets

Windows NT also includes four multiuser applets. They are called multiuser because they can be used by a workgroup as well as by a single individual.

For example, although the Windows 95 Clipboard enables you to exchange data between applications on a single desktop, the Windows NT ClipBook Viewer enables you to exchange data between desktops as well. The following sections look at the four Windows NT multiuser applets: ClipBook Viewer, Mail, Chat, and Schedule+.

ClipBook Viewer

Windows NT users probably work daily with more applications on their desktop than do users of most other operating systems (especially those that do not support multitasking).

A key factor is the ease at which data exchange can be carried out in the Windows NT environment. Windows NT uses a storage area known as the *Clipboard,* which enables you to send data from one application and insert a copy of that data into other applications.

Windows NT 3.*x* has a utility, called the Clipboard Viewer, to view the contents of the Clipboard. Windows NT provides a much more powerful tool: the *ClipBook Viewer,* which is an expanded workgroup version of the Windows 95 Clipboard Viewer.

Although you can use the ClipBook Viewer to view, save, and delete data contained in the Clipboard, you also can use it to exchange data between desktops within your workgroup.

Note The actual storage area for your data is not the ClipBook Viewer. The Clipboard is a much more ethereal entity: a class of Application Programming Interface (API) functions located in the USER library that manage the exchange of data between applications. The ClipBook Viewer is simply a window to that data.

Using the Clipboard

Nearly all Windows applications use the Clipboard. To use it, you need to choose one of three commands found under the Edit menu. These commands are described as follows:

- Cut removes the selection from the active window and places it in the Clipboard.
- Copy duplicates the selection from the active window and places it in the Clipboard.
- Paste inserts the contents of the Clipboard into the active window at the position of the cursor.

Tip If you are cutting and pasting using options in the Edit menu, you are wasting time. The much easier way is to use the following key combinations:

- Ctrl+C to copy the highlighted text
- Ctrl+X to cut the highlighted text
- Ctrl+V to paste the copied or cut text at the current location of the cursor.

Although these keystrokes are far more efficient, not all applications support them. For those applications that do not support these keystrokes, see if you can configure the keyboard entries so you can implement these keystrokes.

The capability to exchange data between Windows NT applications is not as simple as it may appear. To understand this complexity, think about the unique data types of the applications you use (see table 3.2).

Table 3.2
Variety of Available Data Types

Application	Works Primarily With
Word for Windows	Formatted text or Ami Pro
Notepad	Unformatted text
WordPerfect for DOS	OEM text
Excel or Quattro	Spreadsheet data (including Pro for Windows numbers and formulas)
Paintbrush	Bit-mapped graphics
Micrografx Draw	Vector graphics or Aldus Freehand
Microsoft Sound System	Sound

The variety of data types that exists between applications can lead to some potential problems. For instance, how can you transfer formatted text from WordPerfect for Windows to Notepad (which accepts only unformatted text)? If you have ever tried to open up a WordPerfect file (or another word processing file) with Notepad (or another text editor), you know that the result is garbled: text is sandwiched between formatting specifications.

Does this same logic carry over to Clipboard data exchange between WordPerfect and Notepad? No. WordPerfect data is not pasted as unintelligible text into Notepad because of the way in which the source application (WordPerfect), the Clipboard, and the receiving application (Notepad) work together.

Note The contents of the Clipboard are always treated as a single unit. You can never paste part of the Clipboard contents into a document.

When you copy data to the Clipboard, the source application sends data in as many formats as it is able to send. For example, among the formats WordPerfect transfers to the Clipboard is text (consisting of unformatted characters). Notepad is able to accept the WordPerfect data because it also supports text format, and is thus able to paste it correctly into a document.

The source application ultimately is in control of the way the data is formatted. The source application determines the type of format to support; the receiving application makes a determination about which format to accept when it pastes the data. As a result, some of the formatting or information on the data may be lost if the same data formats are not supported in the receiving application.

There is no ceiling on the amount of data you can store in the Clipboard. In fact, you are limited only by the amount of memory your computer has. As a result, imagine the lag on system resources that would result if the source application had to supply the Clipboard with multiple formats of the same data. To get around this problem, most applications tell the Clipboard which types of formats they support, and furnish data in that format when a receiving application requests it from the Clipboard.

Note You have no control over the formats being copied and pasted. The source application determines which formats to send to the Clipboard; the receiving application looks at the available formats and accepts the highest available format. In other words, you cannot force Notepad to accept RTF—Notepad alone makes that determination.

Using the Clipboard Window

When you start the ClipBook Viewer by double-clicking on its icon in the Main group, the ClipBook Viewer appears with two child windows: Local ClipBook and Clipboard.

Use the Clipboard window to work with data on your desktop. Remember that the Clipboard window is not the Clipboard—it is only a window showing the contents of the Clipboard. As a result, the ClipBook Viewer does not need to be running to be able to use the Clipboard.

You can perform the following tasks by using the Clipboard window:

- **Clearing the contents of the Clipboard.** To delete the contents of the Clipboard, activate the Clipboard window and choose the Delete option from the Edit menu or press the Del key. You are asked to confirm this deletion by clicking on the Yes button in a message box.

  An alternative method of clearing the contents of the Clipboard does not require you to open the ClipBook Viewer at all. Instead, it can be done within the application in which you are working.

  For example, if you are in a word-processing application, select a space, and then choose the Copy command from the Edit menu. The space is inserted into the Clipboard, overwriting its previous contents.

- **Viewing data in different formats.** The View menu for the Clipboard window lists the data formats sent by the source application to the Clipboard. To change the display of the data, select one of the formats from the list. You will notice that Default Format is initially checked. This setting signifies that the Clipboard window has automatically selected the format being displayed from the list of available formats. If the source application is running, Default Format displays the contents of the Clipboard window in the format preferred by the source application. If it is not running, the ClipBook Viewer selects the best format left available.

- **Saving the contents of the Clipboard.** You may need to save data in the Clipboard for a later time. There are two ways to save Clipboard data.

  You can save the contents of the Clipboard as a page to the Local ClipBook, which is a permanent storage area for data that you can recall later or share with other workgroup members. To save to the Local ClipBook, select the Local ClipBook window and choose the Paste option from the Edit menu. In a dialog box, you are asked to name the page you are creating, and you have the option to declare it as a shared item (available for use by others). Click on the OK button.

  You cannot save formatted text in the Local ClipBook or as a CLP file. When you paste the formatted text into a Local ClipBook page or save it as a CLP file, it immediately is converted to text format (even if the source application is still running).

  You also can save the contents of the Clipboard to a Clipboard file (as in Windows 95). To do so, choose the Save As option from the File menu. Enter a filename in the Save As dialog box, and click on OK. Clipboard files have a default extension of CLP.

Under most circumstances, you will want to use the Local ClipBook to store contents of the Clipboard. The Local ClipBook enables you to view and share such data much more easily than by working with CLP files.

When you shut down a Windows NT session, Windows NT saves any contents remaining in the Clipboard as a CLP file. You can access that data during a later session.

Using the Local ClipBook

The Local ClipBook is a centralized storage location of Clipboard items. Each separate entry in the Local ClipBook is called a *page*. Pages can be viewed in a list (by choosing the Table of Contents option from the View menu), in Thumbnail view (by choosing the Thumbnails option), or as a display of their actual contents (by choosing the Full Page option).

Figure 3.5 shows the Local ClipBook, displaying its pages in Thumbnail view.

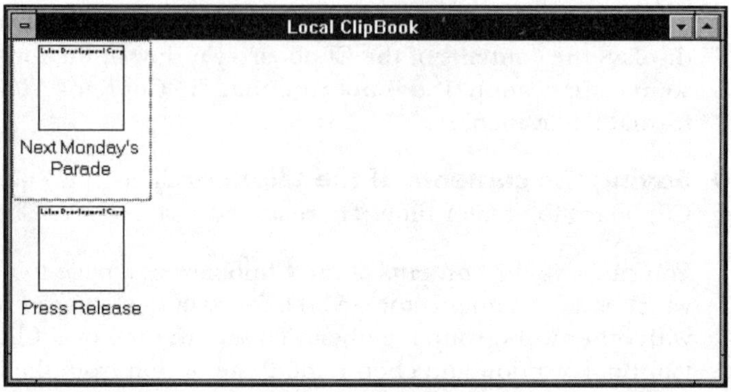

Figure 3.5
The Local ClipBook.

Sharing Data by Using ClipBook

Although the ClipBook Viewer is a useful and powerful tool for an individual desktop, it also can be used to exchange data between desktops. Because all members of your workgroup that run Windows NT have their own ClipBooks, you can access remote data from their ClipBooks, and others can access your Local ClipBook.

Sharing Data from Your Local ClipBook

To enable other users to share your local data, check the Share Item Now box as you paste a new page into your Local ClipBook. If you check the share box, a second dialog appears for you to set specific options.

- **Start Application on Connect.** Checking the Start Application on Connect box causes the source application to start whenever another user accesses this data. This option is useful when creating dynamic links between applications.
- **Run Minimized.** Checking the Run Minimized box forces it to run in a minimized state.
- **Permissions.** Clicking on the Permissions button displays the ClipBook Page Permissions dialog box. In this dialog box, you can set the type of access you want other users to have to the ClipBook page. You can designate the following levels of access: Full Control, Change, Read and Link, Read, and No Access.

After setting these options, other users can connect to, and work with data in, your ClipBook.

Accessing Remote ClipBook Data

You can access shared data on other users' computers and copy it to your Clipboard. To do so, you need to connect to the remote computer's ClipBook by choosing the Connect option from the File menu.

In the Select Computer dialog box, specify the computer you want to connect to by entering the name or selecting a name from the Computers list. After clicking on the OK button, a new window opens in your ClipBook Viewer window, displaying the remote ClipBook.

Note You work with the shared pages of the remote ClipBook in the same way that you work with your Local ClipBook.

To disconnect from another computer, choose the Disconnect option from the File menu.

Mail

One of the best business tools of the information age is electronic mail (e-mail). The use of e-mail within offices can make business communication much more efficient and useful than past forms of written communication.

An e-mail package is a standard element of a typical local area network. Windows NT includes Mail, which is a simplified version of Microsoft Mail. Mail enables you to send and receive electronic mail (both text messages and files) across your workgroup.

Setting Up Mail

To run Mail, use the following procedure.

1. Double-click on its icon in the Main group.

   As Mail loads up for the first time, it prompts you to designate a post office.

Note A post office contains information about user accounts for a workgroup and also functions as a depository for the workgroup's messages.

You can create a new post office or connect to an existing one. If the administrator has not already established an account for you in the post office, you need to create the account.

Note A post office is used by the workgroup, not by a single individual. Thus, all workgroup members have mailboxes within a central postoffice.

2. Typically, a post office has already been set up for your use by the administrator. If so, choose the Connect to an Existing Postoffice in the Welcome to Mail dialog box.

   The Network Disk Resources dialog box appears.

3. Select the desired post office by typing its path in the Network Path text box.

   Alternatively, you can locate the appropriate path by selecting a computer from the top box and the desired path in the lower box.

4. After clicking on the OK button, Mail asks if you currently have an account in the postoffice. If so, click on the Yes button and you are prompted for your password. If you do not have an existing account, click on the No button.

   A dialog box appears, asking for the following information about you:

   - **Name.** Enter your full name (up to 30 characters in length). [Required]
   - **Mailbox.** Enter a name (up to 10 characters) that you will use as a logon name to Mail. It is recommended that you use your Windows NT user name to avoid the necessity of remembering several user names. [Required]
   - **Password.** Enter a password (up to 8 characters) for use as you start Mail. Be sure to choose a password that you can remember. [Required]
   - **Phone #1.** Enter your primary phone number.
   - **Phone #2.** Enter a secondary phone number.
   - **Office.** Enter your office number or location identifier (up to 32 characters).
   - **Department.** Enter your department name (up to 32 characters).
   - **Notes.** Enter any additional information in this field (up to 128 characters).

5. After entering this information, click on the OK button.

   Mail displays the Inbox window. You are now ready to begin using Mail.

Note If you do not connect to an existing post office, you can create a new post office by choosing the Create a new Workgroup Post office option from the Welcome to Mail dialog box. You are required to administer the post office if you create it, however.

Sending a Message

To send a message to one or more users on your network, click on the Compose button from the Mail window, or choose the Compose Note option from the Mail menu. The Send Note window appears, as shown in figure 3.6.

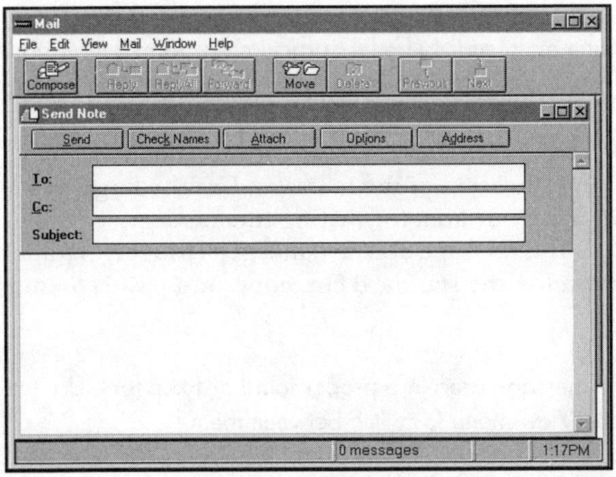

Figure 3.6
The Send Note window.

When you send a message, you have to define the following three elements:

- **Recipient.** Declare the users to which you want to address the message. You can send a message directly to other workgroup members or send it as a carbon copy (cc:).

Note A carbon copy (cc:) is a carryover from traditional written business communications, in which a copy of a letter is sent to all interested parties.

Enter the user name(s) of the person(s) in the To text box. If you want to view an address list of users in the workgroup, click on the Address button. The Address dialog box appears.

Select the name of one or more persons from the list, and click on the To button. (Alternatively, you can double-click on a name in the Directory box.) After you have selected the appropriate names, click on the OK button to return to the Send Note window.

If you want to send a carbon copy of the message to another user, enter the user name in the Cc text box. You can click on the Address button to add user names to the cc: list as well.

Tip Move between fields in the Send Note window by pressing the Tab key or by using your mouse to click on a new field. The Enter key is not used for this purpose.

- **Subject.** Declare a subject of the message so that the recipient understands the message's basic purpose and content before she reads it. Enter the subject for the message in the Subject text box.

Tip Keep in mind that e-mail tends to be less structured or formal than standard paper letters. Because you typically are sending text, formatting and page layout is immaterial.

- **Message.** Enter the actual text of the message. Use the large box at the bottom of the window as your area for writing the message. The actual text-editing capabilities in the message area are meager (roughly parallel to Notepad), but you can use the standard cut, copy, and paste commands.

Tip You can view the message area in a proportional or fixed font. Use the Change Font option on the **View** menu to switch between them.

Before sending the message, you may want to set options for the message. Click on the Options button to display the Options dialog box. Set the desired options, as follows:

- **Return receipt.** If this box is checked, you will be notified when the message recipient(s) reads the message.
- **Save sent messages.** If this box is checked, Mail saves a copy of your message for you. This option enables you to keep a log of your correspondence.
- **Priority.** Electronic messages can have priority levels. Set your message to the appropriate level by choosing the High, Normal, or Low options. The recipient of the message sees the priority of the message in his Inbox.

When you have completed the message and set the desired options, click on the Send button to send the message over the network to the mailbox of the addressee.

Reading a Message

When you receive an e-mail message from another workgroup member, it is placed in your Inbox, as shown in figure 3.7.

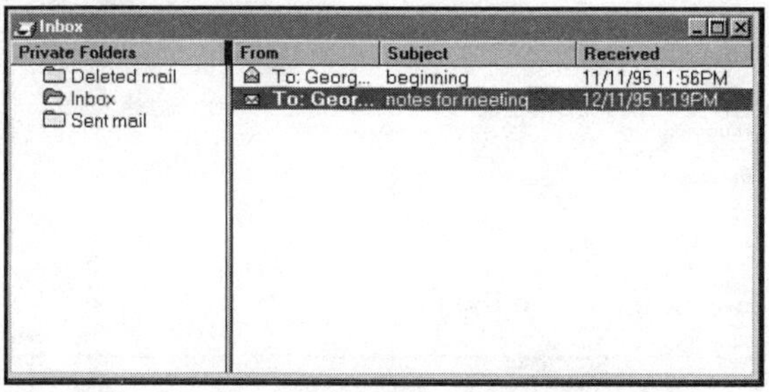

Figure 3.7

An Inbox with incoming mail.

Notice that an unread message has a closed envelope icon beside it. To read the message, double-click on the message entry from the Inbox, or select the entry and press Enter. Your message appears in a message window.

Note The left side of the Inbox displays a list of available folders. You can store your e-mail in a variety of folders, just as you store written correspondence in a filing cabinet.

To view the contents of a folder, click on the appropriate folder icon. Also, by double-clicking on the button at the top of the window, you can switch between private and shared (public) folders.

Responding to a Message

After you read an e-mail message, you might want to respond to that message. Instead of having to create a new message and then reenter the recipient name and subject, you can reply to the existing message.

To reply, click on the Reply button from the toolbar, or choose Reply from the Mail menu. The message window appears (see fig. 3.8).

Mail automatically addresses the letter, adds `"RE: "` to the subject of the message, and provides the original text of the message in the message area below a line.

When you choose the Reply command, your response is sent only to the person who sent you the message. If other users are receiving carbon copies of the message, you probably want to send your reply to them as well. To do this, click on the Reply All button, or choose Reply to All from the Mail menu.

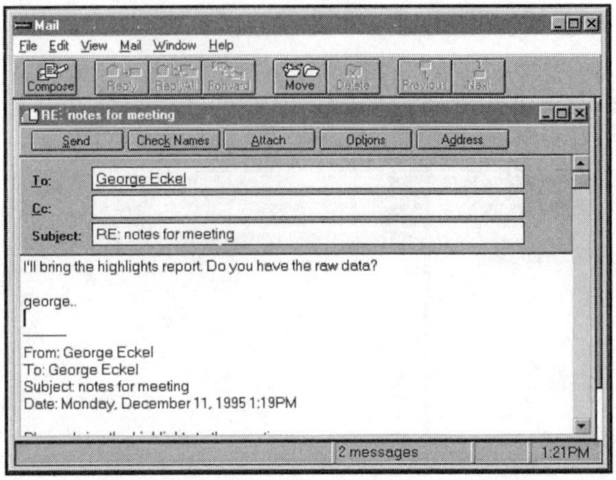

Figure 3.8

Replying to a message.

Removing Messages

To delete messages from your mailbox, select the desired message from the Inbox list, and click the Delete button on the toolbar. Mail moves the message to the Deleted mail folder (see fig. 3.9), where it is deleted as you exit Mail.

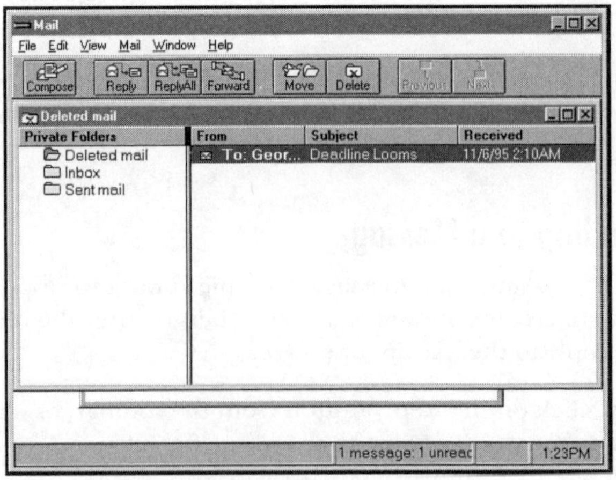

Figure 3.9

Deleted messages are placed in the Deleted mail folder.

If you decide to undelete the message before you exit Mail, click on the Move button to move the message to a different folder.

Chat

Chat is a tool you can use to have a "live" conversation with another workgroup member over the network. To run Chat, double-click on the Chat icon in the Accessories group. The Chat window appears, as shown in figure 3.10.

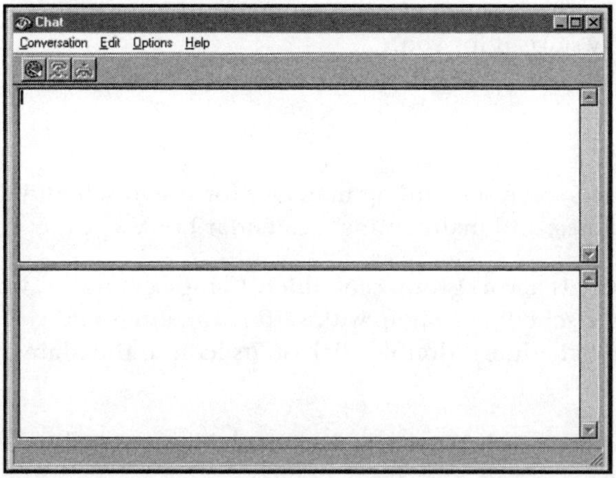

Figure 3.10

The Chat window.

Think of Chat as a different type of phone, and a Chat conversation as a different kind of phone call. To conduct a Chat conversation, do the following:

- **Call another user.** Call another workgroup member by clicking on the Dial button on the toolbar or by choosing the Dial option from the Conversation menu. Choose the computer name of the person you are trying to call, and click on OK.

  Chat then calls the computer you choose, and waits for the person whom you are calling to answer. The status bar at the bottom of the Chat window notifies you of the call's status.

Tip Think of the computer name as a phone number, because each phone number has a physical location to which it is associated.

- **Conduct a conversation.** If a user answers the Chat request, the caller can begin typing in the top window while the receiver types in the bottom window. A conversation need not be unidirectional; you both can type information simultaneously if needed.

- **Hang up.** When you are finished with the conversation, you or the other workgroup member are free to hang up and terminate the conversation. To do so, click on the Hangup button from the toolbar, or choose the Hangup option from the Conversation menu. When the person with whom you are conversing hangs up, you are notified by Mail in the status bar.

If another workgroup member calls you and requests an online Chat conversation, you can answer the call by clicking on the Answer button from the toolbar or by choosing the Answer option from the Conversation menu. If Chat is not open, Windows NT automatically starts it for you.

Schedule

Schedule+ is a miniature personal scheduling manager for use in scheduling appointments and tasks, jotting notes, and maintaining a calendar book.

Schedule+ also can be used as a workgroup scheduler. Using Schedule+, workgroup members can have a public schedule to help with setting meetings and viewing others' schedules. To run Schedule+, double-click on its icon in the Main group.

Note Schedule+ is much more advanced than the limited Calendar applet provided in Windows NT 3.*x*.

Schedule+ uses the same user name and password as Mail. If you already have established these in Mail, you do not have to do so again in Schedule+. Instead, enter your user name and password in the Password dialog box. The Schedule+ Appointment List window appears (see fig. 3.11).

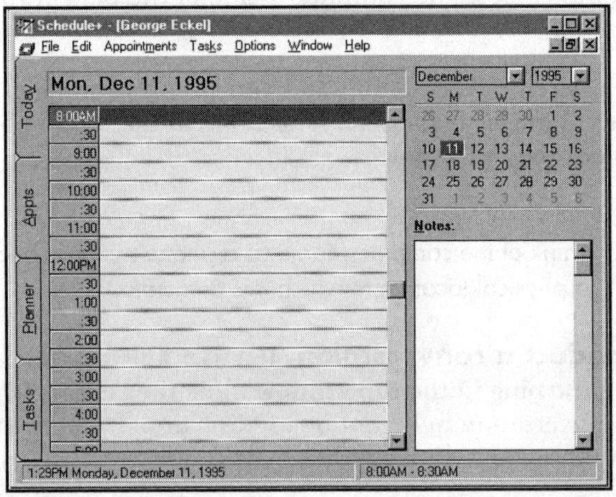

Figure 3.11
The Schedule+ window.

The Schedule+ window can be divided up into the following four areas:

- **Tabs.** The tabs on the left of the window enable you to view different pages of Schedule+. Click on one of the four tabs to switch between page views.
- **Calendar.** The monthly calendar shows the current month by default. To view a different date, select the appropriate month and year from the list boxes above the calendar, and click on the date in the calendar.
- **Daily schedule.** The main part of the window is a daily schedule for the date specified above it (and in the calendar beside it). Enter appointments and block out activities in this box.
- **Notes.** Enter any miscellaneous comments related to the current day in this box.

The following tasks explain how to accomplish primary tasks using the four areas in Schedule+.

Scheduling an Appointment

To schedule an appointment in Schedule+, designate the block of time for the activity by selecting an initial time (12:00 p.m., for example), then drag the mouse to the end time (2:00 p.m.).

From the Appointments menu, choose the New Appointments option. The Appointment dialog box appears (see fig. 3.12).

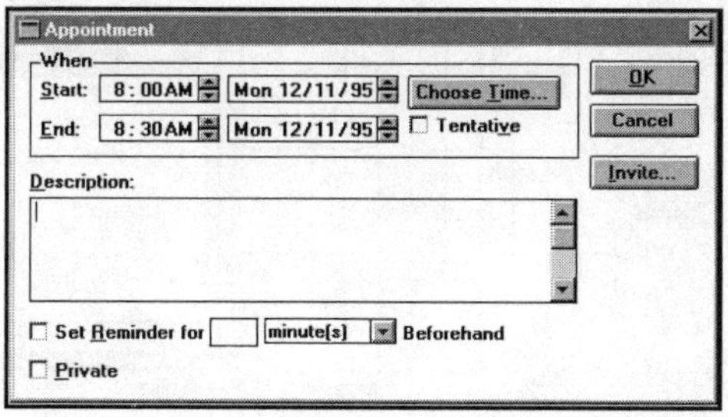

Figure 3.12

The Appointment dialog box.

Set the following appointment details in this dialog box:

- **When.** In the When box, your Start and End times for the appointment already have been set. Modify them if necessary. You can declare the appointment as tentative by checking the Tentative box.

- **Description.** Enter text in the Description box to describe the appointment. Use as much space as necessary. Schedule+ places this text in the time block that you specify in your daily schedule of the main Schedule+ window.
- **Reminder.** Check the Set Reminder for check box if you want Schedule+ to issue a reminder before the time of an appointment. Enter the amount of time before you want the reminder issued in the space provided.
- **Private.** If you want to keep the description of your appointment private from other workgroup members, check the Private box.
- **Invite.** Click on the Invite button to invite other workgroup members to attend the appointment. In the Select Attendees dialog box, choose the persons you want to invite from the post office list.

You do not need to enter information in each field.

Using the Planner

The Planner window (see fig. 3.13) displays the times you and other workgroup members have set appointments.

Figure 3.13

The Planner window.

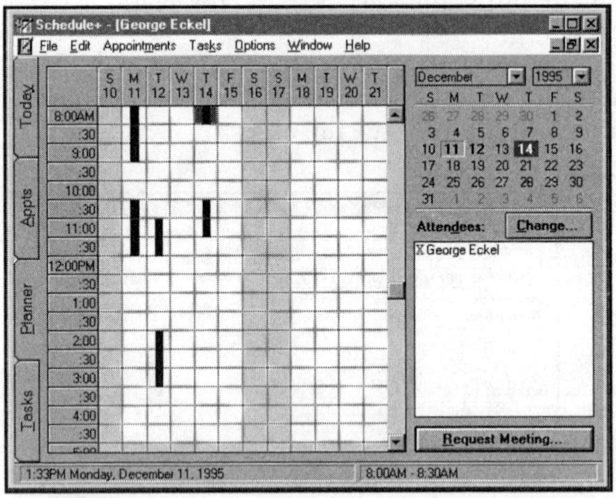

The Planner window can be divided into the following four areas:

- **Tabs.** The tabs on the left of the window enable you to view different pages of Schedule+. Click on one of the four tabs to switch between page views.
- **Time slots.** The main part of the window is an appointment grid, displaying the time slots of set appointments. To view an appointment, double-click on its

time slot in the Planner window. Schedule+ displays the Appointment Book window of the person who scheduled the appointment.

- **Calendar.** The monthly calendar shows the current month by default. To view a different date, select the appropriate month and year from the list boxes above the calendar, and click on the date in the calendar with your mouse.

- **Attendees.** The Attendees box displays the names of the workgroup members whose appointments are shown in Schedule+. To change the list, click on the Change button, and choose the desired workgroup members from the Select Attendees dialog box. In addition, if you want to send a meeting request to each of the attendees, click on the Request Meeting button.

Using the Task List

You can use the Task List to list and prioritize activities you need to perform. Access the Task List by clicking on the Tasks tab of the Schedule+ window (see fig. 3.14).

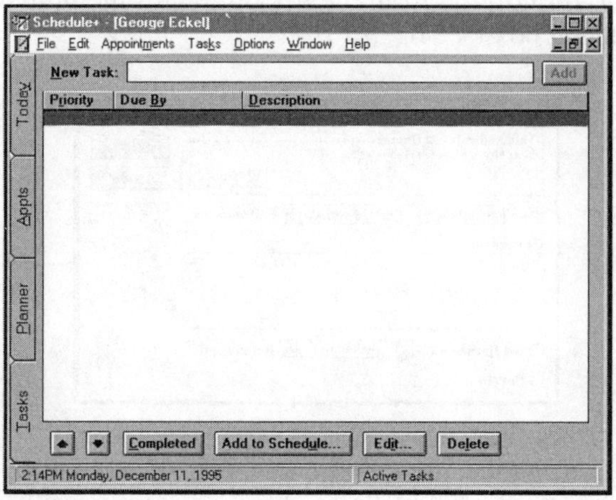

Figure 3.14
The Tasks window.

The Task List has the following options:

- **Add task.** To add a new task, enter its description in the New Task text box and click on the Add button (or press Enter). The new task is added to the Task List.

- **Edit task.** You can edit a task after it has been placed on the Task List by double-clicking on the list item (or by selecting the item and clicking on the Edit button). The Task dialog box appears, enabling you to change the task's description, project, due date, and priority.

- **Add project.** Schedule+ enables you to group tasks by project. To add a project, choose the New Project option from the Tasks menu. In the Project dialog box, enter a project name in the Name text box. Check the Private box to prevent other workgroup members from seeing the contents of this list.
- **Completed task.** When a task is completed, remove it from the list by selecting it and clicking on the Completed button.

You can master these tasks easily and thereby gain some control over projects you embark on.

Scheduling a Recurring Appointment

Schedule+ can automatically schedule a recurring appointment (a board meeting every Friday at 10:00 a.m., for example) for you. Click on the Appts tab, and set the desired date by using the calendar. Next, select the desired time block by dragging your mouse from the starting time to the ending time.

Choose the New Recurring Appt option from the Appointments menu to display the Recurring Appointment dialog box (see fig. 3.15).

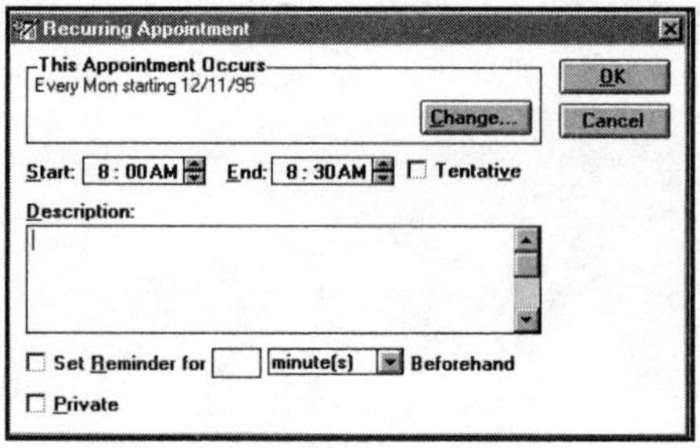

Figure 3.15
The Recurring Appointment dialog box.

Click on the Change button to display the Change Recurrence dialog box. Select the desired pattern by setting its occurrence (daily, weekly, biweekly, monthly, yearly), day of week, and duration.

Using Administrator Tools

A new set of applets, called Administrator Tools, is provided in Windows NT to help administrators configure and monitor their Windows NT networks. These tools, discussed in the following sections, include the Disk Administrator, User Manager, Performance Monitor, Event Viewer, and Backup.

Note These utilities are not for everyone's use—they are available only to users with administrator-level rights on the network.

Disk Administrator

The Disk Administrator is a powerful tool that is used to configure local and networked hard drives. It enables you to work with any physical or logical FAT (File Allocation Table, used by DOS), HPFS (High Performance File System, used by OS/2), and NTFS (NT File System) drives. It does not, however, currently support drives compressed using MS-DOS 6.0's DoubleSpace.

To run Disk Administrator, double-click on the Disk Administrator icon in the Administrative Tools group. The Disk Administrator window appears, as shown in figure 3.16.

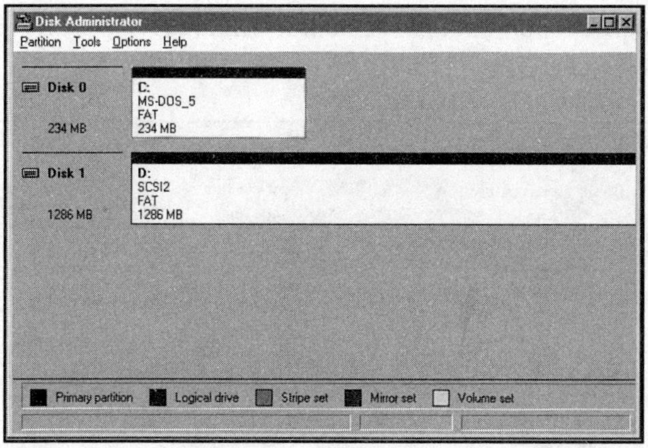

Figure 3.16
The Disk Administrator.

Disk Administrator enables you to perform many of the same tasks as DOS's FDISK utility. Although it may seem strange to perform such low-level functions on your disk in a graphical environment, Disk Administrator is much more powerful than its DOS counterpart.

Note Disk Administrator does not provide the capability to convert FAT drives to NTFS. This command must be performed by using the command-line utility CONVERT. Formatting a drive must also be performed by entering **FORMAT** at the command prompt.

Compressing Files

The compress utility can compress and uncompress files residing in NTFS partitions. Compression ratios vary according to the type of file. Text files, for example, often do not compress much—perhaps 1.5 to 1. Graphics files, however, can often compress a great deal—perhaps 9 to 1.

To compress files on your NTFS partitions, use one of the following procedures:

1. In the File Manager, hold down the Ctrl key and use the mouse to highlight all of the files you want to compress.
2. Click on the Compress option in the File menu.

Or

1. In the File Manager, hold down the Ctrl key and use the mouse to highlight all of the files you want to compress.
2. Click on the Properties option in the File menu. Windows NT displays the Properties dialog box, as shown in figure 3.17.

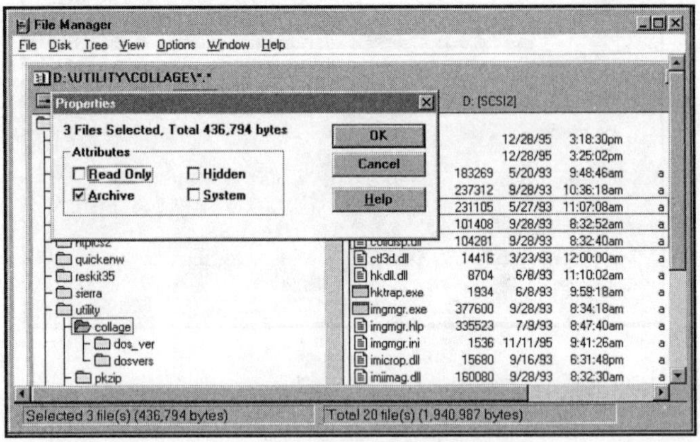

Figure 3.17

The Properties window.

3. Click on the Compressed check box.

User Manager

User Manager is used by the administrator to manage user accounts on the Windows NT network. To run User Manager, double-click on the User Manager icon in the Administrative Tools group. The User Manager window appears, as shown in figure 3.18.

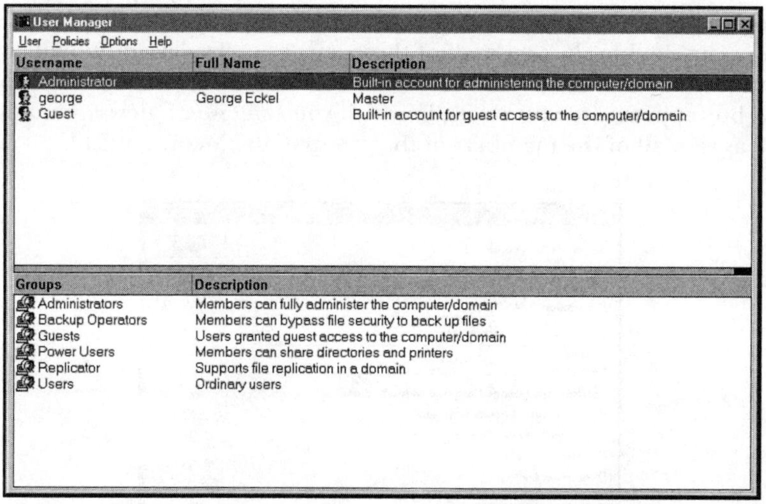

Figure 3.18
The User Manager.

The top portion of the window displays a list of user names for the entire system. Data tracked includes the following:

- **Username.** Refers to the logon name that you enter as you log on to the system.
- **Full Name.** Used to enter the complete name of the user. Although this data is not used by Windows NT, it is helpful for the administrator to work with full names rather than cryptic user names.
- **Description.** Used to enter optional comments about a particular user (such as title or position in the company). This is another field not required by Windows NT.

You can view or modify additional information on a specific user by double-clicking on the entry in the Username list. The User Properties dialog box appears, as shown in figure 3.19.

Although the administrator can modify some of the settings, such as Full Name and Description, she cannot change or view the password. A password is proprietary to each individual user.

When a new account has no password, or an existing account's password has expired, the administrator can add a password to the account. The administrator can view or modify additional information about the user by clicking on the Groups or Profile button. As you finish working with a user account, click on the OK button to return to the User Manager window.

The lower portion of the User Manager window lists the user groups that are defined for the system. You can double-click on each of these entries to display additional information about each group. When you double-click on an entry, the Local Group Properties dialog box appears (see fig. 3.20), in which you can enter a description of the group as well as view all of the members of the group in the Members list.

Figure 3.19

The User Properties dialog box.

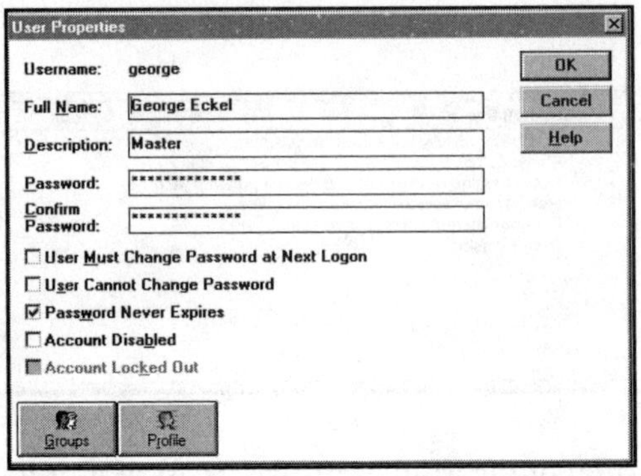

Figure 3.20

The Local Group Properties dialog box.

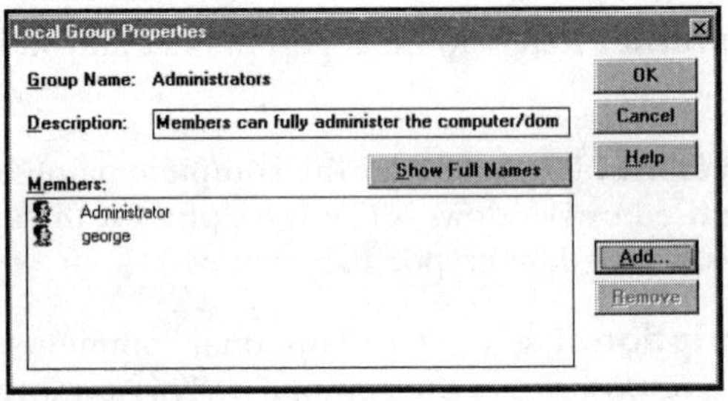

Add additional users to the group by clicking on the **A**dd button. Delete a user from the group by selecting a user name from the Members list and clicking on the **R**emove button.

Performance Monitor

Performance Monitor enables the administrator to track the performance of the system. To run Performance Monitor, double-click on the Performance Monitor icon in the Administrative Tools group. The Performance Monitor window appears, as shown in figure 3.21.

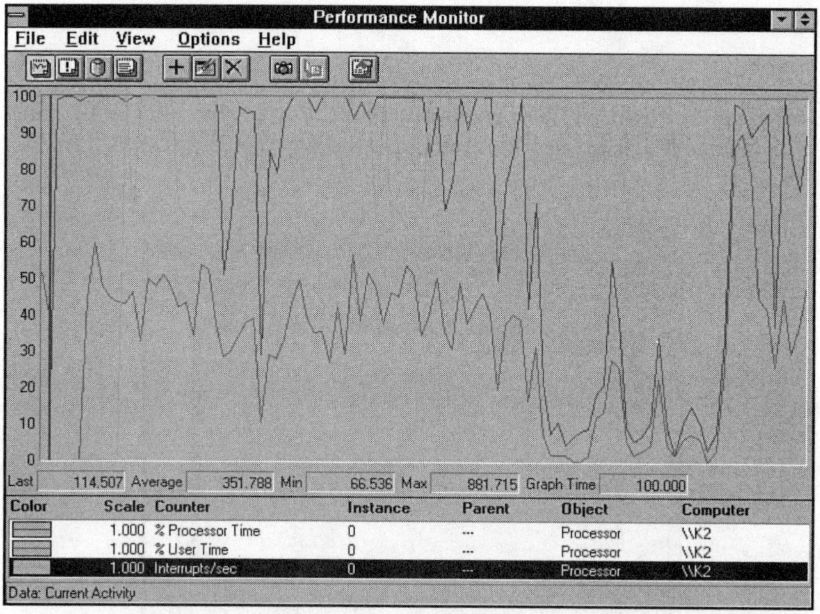

Figure 3.21

The Performance Monitor.

Event Viewer

Event Viewer is another tool that can be used by the administrator to track system-operation logs kept by Windows NT. The system logs document-system events (for example, errors and warnings encountered), application events (such as crashes), and security events (such as invalid password entries).

To run Event Viewer, double-click on the Event Viewer icon in the Administrative Tools group. The Event Viewer window appears, as shown in figure 3.22.

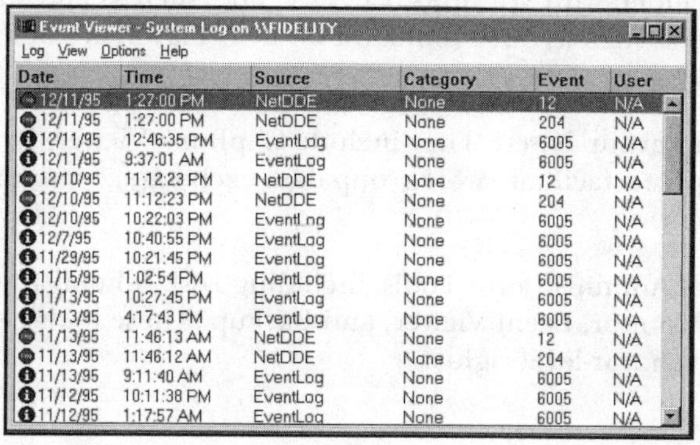

Date	Time	Source	Category	Event	User
12/11/95	1:27:00 PM	NetDDE	None	12	N/A
12/11/95	1:27:00 PM	NetDDE	None	204	N/A
12/11/95	12:46:35 PM	EventLog	None	6005	N/A
12/11/95	9:37:01 AM	EventLog	None	6005	N/A
12/10/95	11:12:23 PM	NetDDE	None	12	N/A
12/10/95	11:12:23 PM	NetDDE	None	204	N/A
12/10/95	10:22:03 PM	EventLog	None	6005	N/A
12/7/95	10:40:55 PM	EventLog	None	6005	N/A
11/29/95	10:21:45 PM	EventLog	None	6005	N/A
11/15/95	1:02:54 PM	EventLog	None	6005	N/A
11/13/95	10:27:45 PM	EventLog	None	6005	N/A
11/13/95	4:17:43 PM	EventLog	None	6005	N/A
11/13/95	11:46:13 AM	NetDDE	None	12	N/A
11/13/95	11:46:12 AM	NetDDE	None	204	N/A
11/13/95	9:11:40 AM	EventLog	None	6005	N/A
11/12/95	10:11:38 PM	EventLog	None	6005	N/A
11/12/95	1:17:57 AM	EventLog	None	6005	N/A

Figure 3.22

The Event Viewer.

Backup

The final tool is Backup, which, as its name implies, is used to back up and restore volumes, directories, and individual files. To run Backup, double-click on the Backup icon in the Administrative Tools group. The Backup window appears, as shown in figure 3.23.

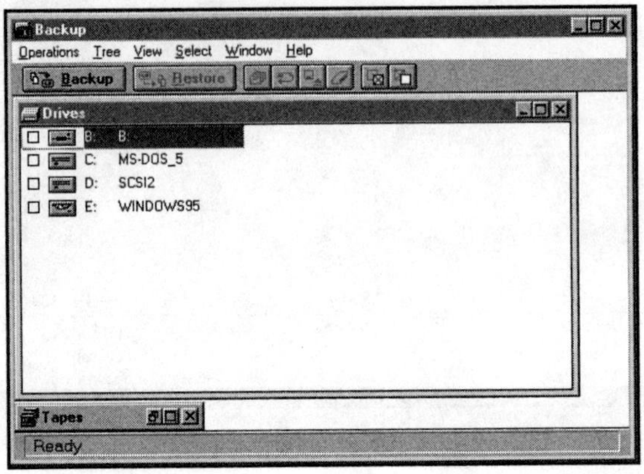

Figure 3.23

The Backup window.

Summary

Although the acceptance of the Windows NT operating system is not based on the applets that are included with it, these mini-applications do play an important role for users of the environment. This chapter looked at the applets that come with Windows NT, and divided them into three groups: single user, multiuser, and administrative.

The single-user applets make up the largest group of NT applets. Most in this group are identical to those included with Windows NT 3.*x*. Some, such as File Manager, have been enhanced; a few, such as 3270 Emulator and CD Player, are new applets designed for Windows NT.

Multiuser applets are workgroup-based. They include ClipBook Viewer, Mail, Chat, and Schedule+. These applets facilitate workgroup data exchange, communication, and schedule coordination.

The final group is a set of Administrative Tools, including Disk Administrator, User Manager, Performance Monitor, Event Viewer, and Backup. These tools can be used only by users with administrator-level rights.

CHAPTER 4

Learning How to Perform Basic Tasks with Windows NT

Paradoxically, as operating systems have become much more powerful and architecturally complex, they also have become easier to use. Today's state-of-the-art operating systems (particularly Windows NT and OS/2) are graphical environments, in which you use a pointing device to perform many actions instead of typing arcane instructions at a command prompt. New Windows NT users should take comfort in the fact that the graphical nature of Windows NT makes it easy to navigate and use.

This chapter begins a discussion of the very basic tools you use when you interact with the Windows NT interface. An *interface* is what an operating system uses to interact with a user.

This chapter also talks about the concept of Common User Access (CUA), by which basic commands (such as opening or printing a file) are done similarly across different applications. The following topics are covered:

- Examining the Windows NT interface
- Using the mouse

- Working with windows and icons
- Performing common Windows tasks
- Introducing WYSIWYG and MDI

Historically, the interface used in most operating system environments has been the *command-line interface* (CLI), and the operating system is represented by the *command prompt* (C:> on most MS-DOS systems, $ on most Unix systems). You enter commands at the command prompt by typing at the keyboard. The prompt tells you that the computer is ready to receive information. To start a program, type the program's name, and press Enter.

In most operating systems, simple file-manipulation commands consist of two words: a verb followed by a noun, as in the MS-DOS command DELETE MYFILE.TST. Commands can be complex (involving other nouns and options), and the command-line interface can be intimidating to the novice user. Although MS-DOS and OS/2 commands are based on the English language, they can appear cryptic (for example, RD stands for Remove Directory in DOS). Unix commands are famous for being cryptic because most consist of such a two-letter abbreviation.

In Windows NT, this verb-noun process is reversed. First, you select the item to be manipulated, then you indicate the action to be performed. The action can involve moving the mouse and clicking the mouse button, selecting an item from a menu, or entering text from the keyboard. In many cases, especially within applications in which the same item is manipulated a number of times, the item already is selected by Windows NT, and you need to specify only the action; for example, in a word processing program, you might highlight a word and then make it bold, italicized, and underlined. The word remains highlighted after you perform each of these actions.

Using a Graphical Interface

As you have learned, Windows NT is a graphical user interface (GUI) that dramatically changes the way in which users interact with the computer. To become comfortable with the Windows NT environment, you must get used to a different way of doing things. Instead of entering commands at a prompt, you use the keyboard or mouse to manipulate symbols on the screen. This collection of symbols is the heart of the Windows NT environment.

As you enter Windows NT after logging on, you see the Windows NT desktop. The term *desktop* often is used to refer to the entire Windows NT environment. Technically, the desktop is the screen background for Windows NT, but the term is used to signify all the things you see when you look at the Windows NT screen (like the items on an office desktop). Each new task is run within individual display areas called *windows*.

Note Many users who are used to DOS and Unix find multiple windows a curiosity because few DOS or Unix programs have exotic options that give you new ways to look at your documents.

If you use a spreadsheet, for example, you can use one window for the data-input area; another window can show the grand totals for the worksheet. As you enter new numbers, you see the effect in terms of total expenditures on the bottom line, even hundreds of rows below. You even can compare two versions of a letter you are writing, or you can keep an outline in one window while writing the body of your text in another.

Using the Mouse

While in Windows NT, most actions are performed by using a mouse or other pointing device. Although there are keyboard equivalents for most mouse actions, they are cumbersome to use. Even though a mouse is not required to run Windows NT, you need a pointing device to be productive in the graphical environment.

For many users of character-based environments, it is difficult to learn to use the mouse. Typically, these users learned how to use the keyboard to interact with the computer. Now, the action of removing their hands from the keys is foreign to their standard way of working. After they work with a mouse for a short period of time, however, the actions become second nature.

Note A single mouse action can replace several commands that you must type and execute individually at the command prompt.

The location of the mouse is represented on-screen by the *pointer* (sometimes described as the *mouse cursor*). The standard pointer is the arrow, as shown in figure 4.1.

The pointer and the mouse move together. By sliding the mouse away from you, you move the pointer up on the display. By pulling the mouse toward you, you move the pointer down on the display. Side-to-side motions move the pointer to the left and right on the display. This activity of changing the location of the mouse pointer is often called *pointing* in Windows NT.

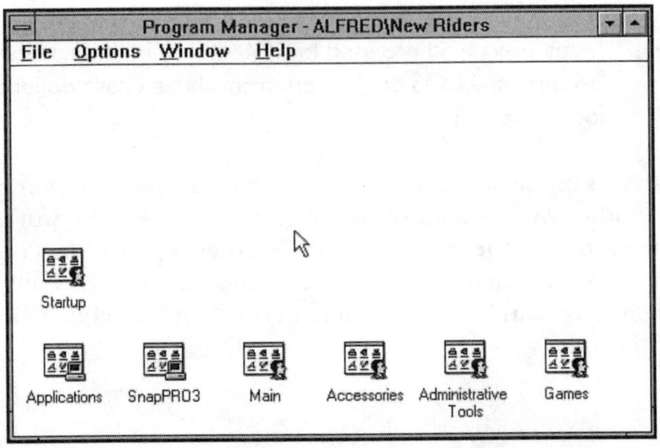

Figure 4.1
The location of the mouse, represented by the arrow pointer.

Besides pointing, there are four other mouse actions; each one has an action associated with it that application programs exploit. These mouse actions are described in the following sections.

Clicking with the Mouse

Mouse actions are performed by using the mouse buttons. In a standard Windows NT environment, the left mouse button is the select button. Depressing and releasing the mouse button is referred to as *clicking* the button. In most situations, clicking the mouse button while the pointer is over an object selects that object, causing it to become active. The item actually is selected when the mouse button is first pressed; releasing the button completes the action.

If you click on a menu name, the menu opens and becomes active. If you click on a menu option, the associated command becomes active, and it executes. If you click on an application icon, it becomes active and displays its Control menu. If you click on a window, it becomes the active window. If you click on a window's workspace, you move the insertion point.

In addition to activating objects on-screen, you also can use the click to execute an action. For example, dialog boxes often have OK and Cancel buttons. By clicking the OK button on the Open dialog box, you open the specified file. If you click the Cancel button instead, the dialog box closes without taking any additional action (that is, opening a file).

Note Because a click action is not performed until you release the mouse button, you can cancel a click action in progress by moving the mouse pointer away from the object before releasing the mouse button.

One mouse click saves you multiple keystrokes when you have to cycle through a list of objects on the screen or move the cursor from the lower-right corner to the upper-left corner. The mouse enables you to be more efficient.

Double-Clicking with the Mouse

Double-clicking is pressing the mouse button twice in rapid succession (usually within one-half of a second). Double-clicking has a rhythm to it, so do not be disappointed if it takes some time to get the hang of it. Double-clicking activates an object and causes it to take a predefined action.

If the two clicks are not done within the time limit, the action is seen as two separate clicks rather than as one double-click. The double-click action typically is used to start applications and open new windows.

Double-clicking on an icon, for example, activates the icon and causes it to open and display the associated window (see fig. 4.2). Each type of icon opens and displays its window differently. It might launch a new application, for instance, or display information present in memory.

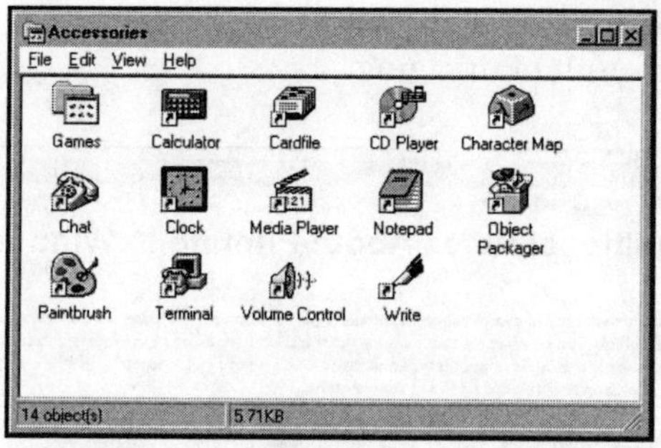

Figure 4.2
The result of double-clicking on the Accessories program-item icon.

Note Double-clicking on the icon on the left side of the title bar selects the Close option in the Control menu. You can exit any window that has an icon in the title bar in this manner.

Dragging an Object

Many actions within the Windows NT environment involve changing the position of an item on-screen by *dragging* the item to a new location. To drag an item, position the pointer over the item, press the mouse button, move the mouse to the new location (while still holding down the mouse button), and then release the mouse button. Each of these steps serves a specific function.

The first item is selected by positioning the pointer over the item and pressing the mouse button. Because the action is not yet completed, the mouse button is not yet released. Moving the mouse moves the items, and when the item is in its new location, the action is completed by releasing the mouse button. Although this combination of actions might seem awkward at first, it quickly becomes a simple task.

Dragging can dramatically affect objects. If you drag the title bar of a window, the entire window moves about on the screen. Dragging a window border changes the window's size. Dragging an icon moves it about on the screen. Dragging the insertion point selects an area of the workspace.

Dragging is like using the arrow-control key combinations in DOS programs. Screen items change position, and you can mark screen blocks for block operations. Using the mouse to perform such actions is faster than using the keyboard, and boosts efficiency. Figure 4.3 shows a result of dragging.

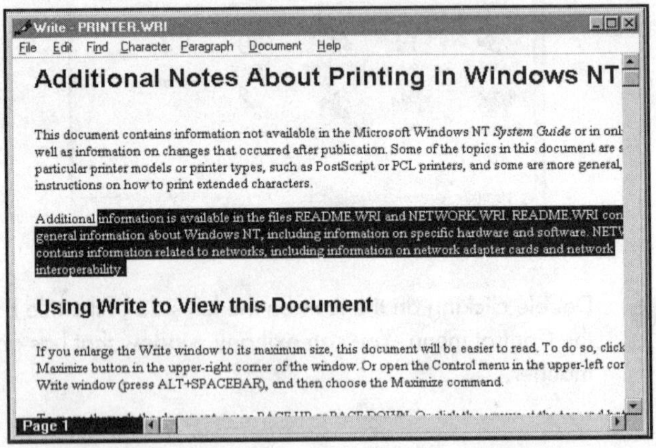

Figure 4.3
The result of dragging on the workspace.

Note Dragging in Windows NT is like using the keyboard to mark screen blocks in programs that run under other, nongraphical operating systems.

Dragging-and-Dropping

The final mouse action is called *dragging-and-dropping*. In this action, you drag an object with the mouse as previously described. The goal of dragging the object is not to change its location on the screen, but to take an action on the object. You drag the object over another object—one that is capable of taking action on the object you are dragging. Then you release the mouse button, dropping the dragged object on its destination. The destination object opens and takes a default action on the dropped object.

File Manager is one application in which you can put drag-and-drop to good use. You can, for example, select a text file from the file list and drag-and-drop it on an open Notepad window; this action causes Notepad to open the text file automatically.

You also can drag-and-drop a file name onto a directory icon to move the file from its current path into the chosen directory. Or you can copy a selected file to another drive by dragging-and-dropping the file name onto a drive icon. Thus, in File Manager, dragging-and-dropping automates an open, move, or copy operation. Dragging-and-dropping enables you to perform very complex processes with a fraction of the effort of typing commands at a command prompt. As a result, you gain in productivity.

Use the following exercise to become familiar with basic mouse actions:

1. Click on the Start button and click on the Programs option.

2. Click on the Accessories program group by double-clicking on the icon labeled Accessories.

3. Select the Notepad icon by moving the mouse, placing the pointer over the icon labeled Notepad, and pressing the select button once. This process is known as *clicking* on the item.

4. Select the Write icon by placing the mouse on the icon and clicking it.

5. Double-click on the Notepad icon. This process opens the Notepad program.

6. Place the pointer at the bottom-right corner of Notepad's window so that the pointer changes to a double diagonal arrow.

7. To resize the Notepad window, drag the window by pressing and holding the select button, moving the mouse to make Notepad's window smaller, and then releasing the select button.

8. Double-click on Notepad's title bar, which is located at the top of the program. It shows the name of the application or document.

9. Click on Notepad's minimize button, which is the button with the dash in the upper-right corner of the Notepad window.

You can see that manipulating items in the Windows NT environment is an easy task when you use the mouse.

Windows NT often uses a three-dimensional appearance for buttons and other screen objects. Usually, these 3-D objects "move" when you click on them with the mouse—indicating that the mouse click is seen by Windows NT.

Using the Mouse Pointer

Within the Windows NT environment, the pointer often changes to indicate the type of action being performed. Figure 4.4 shows several common Windows NT pointers. These pointers inform the user that Windows NT is ready to perform a special type of task.

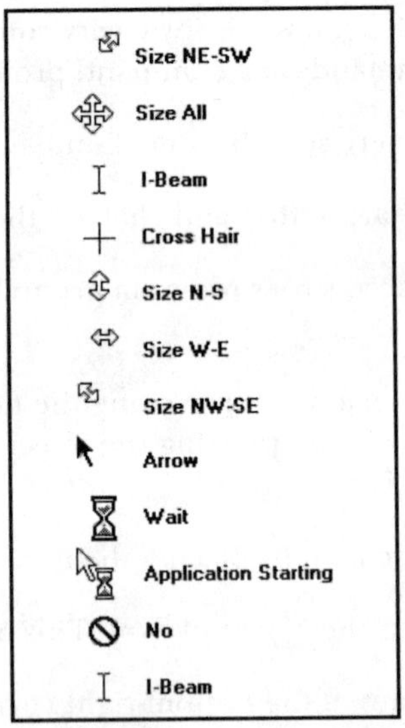

Figure 4.4
Pointer appearance indicates Windows NT's current function.

When resizing an object, the pointer changes to a multiheaded arrow. The directions of the arrows indicate the directions that the object can be moved. When moving an object, the pointer changes to a ghost of the object. A *ghost,* within Windows NT, is an object that is represented with a light gray outline or a special picture.

One of the most common (and least loved) pointers is the hourglass, which appears when Windows NT is performing a task that requires you to wait. Although it is annoying to have to wait, the hourglass lets you know that the system still is functioning.

Note Because Windows NT is a multithreaded and multitasking operating system, a new mouse cursor that combines the arrow and the hourglass has been added. It shows you that the system is busy with one application, but that you are free to continue work with others.

Users familiar with Windows 3.1 also know that the hourglass rarely appears over the background layer of the desktop in Windows NT. Usually it appears only while the cursor is over a busy application. One of the advantages of multithreading and multitasking strategies employed in Windows NT is that you can work with other applications even though one application is busy.

When working with text in Windows NT, the standard pointer is replaced with a steadily flashing dark vertical bar called the *insertion point.* This bar indicates the location at which new text is inserted when you start typing. This mouse pointer looks like a capital I.

A related pointer is referred to as the *I-beam pointer* because of its shape. This mouse pointer tells you where you will move the insertion point if you click at the current location of the mouse. The I-beam appears when you move the mouse pointer over a window in which you can insert text, and tells you that the mouse action you would perform by clicking is the relocation of the insertion point. It also tells you that you can select text by dragging.

The following exercise illustrates the way Windows NT changes the pointer according to the current action. Follow these steps:

1. Select the Notepad window by clicking inside it with the mouse.
2. Place the pointer inside the Notepad window and notice the shape of the pointer. It changes to the I-beam pointer.
3. Move the pointer into the title bar. The pointer changes back to the arrow pointer.
4. Place the pointer on the top window border. The pointer changes to an up/down arrow to indicate window resizing.

You see from this exercise that Windows NT gives you visual clues about the function of the pointer as the task changes. Windows NT also uses the shape of the pointer to give you information about your actions, as is the case with the prevent pointer.

Working with Windows and Application Buttons

As its name suggests, the basic element of the Windows NT interface is a *window*, which is a rectangular area on the screen that displays information from a program. A window can be expanded to cover the entire screen. In this state, the window is said to be *maximized*.

If you no longer need to view the information in the window, but you want to keep it active, you can reduce the window to an *application button* (a small button on the Taskbar). Reducing a window to an application button is referred to as *minimizing* a window. To restore the application button to a window, single click on its application button in the Taskbar. Figure 4.5 shows several common Windows applications as windows and as application buttons in the Taskbar.

Figure 4.5

Program windows and application buttons on the desktop.

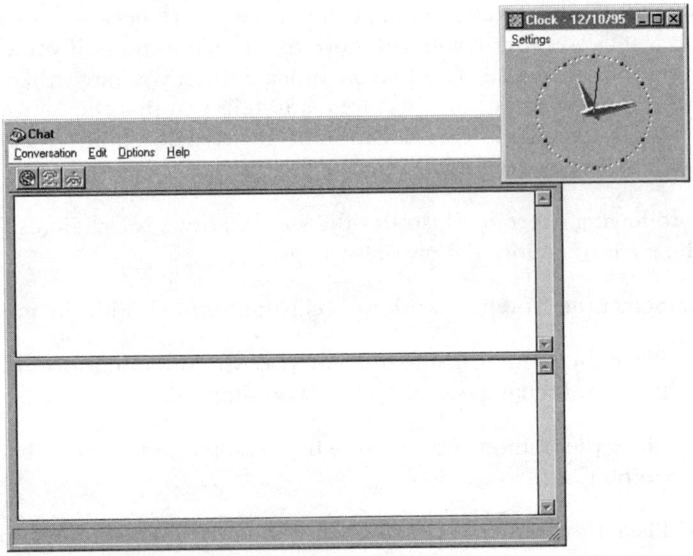

Each Windows NT application has its own window, referred to as a *parent window* or *application window.* The coordination of the parent windows is managed by the Windows NT environment.

Each application may in turn contain windows of its own. These windows, called *child windows* or *document windows,* are managed by the application. The terms *child window* and *parent window* are used when discussing the window's relationships; the terms *application window* and *document window* are used when discussing the window's contents.

Note If an application supports child windows, it is said to have a multiple document interface (MDI). For more information on working with an MDI application, see the discussion later in this chapter.

Individual windows are similar to flexible sheets of paper: you can stack them on top of each other or place them side by side. You can resize windows to display as little or as much of the information as you want. You can change the position or size of the window without changing its content. The view you see through a window is like a landscape being viewed through a video-camera lens; there is a big world out there, but you can see only what is directly in front of the camera.

If you make the view or aperture smaller, you see less of the same view. To see an item that is not in the current view, increase the amount of information in the view (make the view larger). If that does not work, move the camera. If you want to maintain your first view and see another item, get a second camera (open a new window).

Not all of the spreadsheet can be shown within a document window. To view the remainder of the spreadsheet, you can think of moving the window over the part of the spreadsheet that you want to see.

Basic Window Elements

All windows within the Windows NT environment have the same basic set of elements. These elements enable you to manipulate the window's view and its position. Each component is used to perform a specific Windows-management task. As with all actions within Windows NT, each of the tasks associated with managing windows can be accomplished in a number of distinct ways. Figure 4.6 shows these window elements.

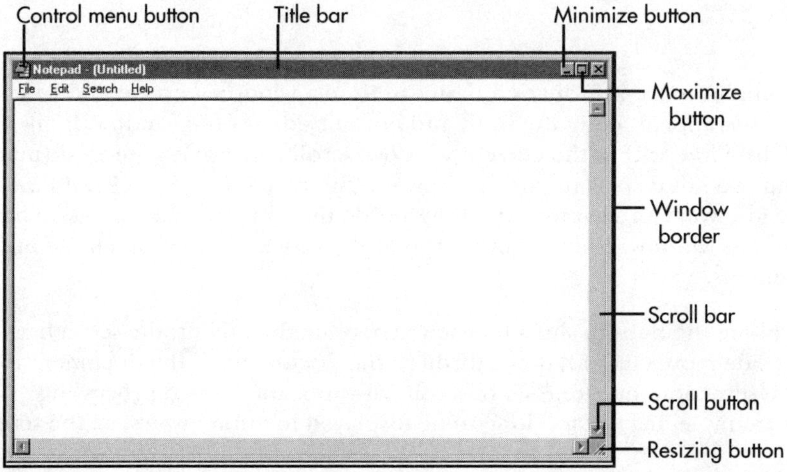

Figure 4.6

An empty Notepad document, showing the basic window elements.

The window components are discussed in the following sections.

Window Border

The *border* around each window can be used to change the size and shape of the window. If you grab the side of the window, you can change only the position of that side. By grabbing a corner, you change the dimensions of both neighboring sides. When you place the mouse on the border or corner, the mouse pointer changes into a double-headed arrow, enabling you to drag the window border to enlarge or shrink the window.

Note The shape of the pointer when it is over a window border indicates the way in which the window can be resized. The pointer changes to a pair of vertical arrows (resize vertically), a pair of horizontal arrows (resize horizontally), or a pair of diagonal arrows (resize diagonally).

The lower-right corner of most windows is an empty square. This square, often called the *resizing button,* also can be used to change the size of the window. Because it is larger than the window border, the resizing button is much easier to grab. You can move the bottom and right sides of the window by dragging the resizing button. When you try to position a window accurately, position the upper-left corner of the window by dragging on the title bar, and then use the resizing button to position the remaining two sides.

Note Not all Windows NT programs provide a resizing button. The Windows NT applets Write and Notepad, for example, do not; Excel and Word for Windows resize in this manner.

Scroll Bars

If a program contains more information than can fit in a window, vertical and horizontal *scroll bars* appear along the right and bottom sides of the window. If all information is displayed within the current window, scroll bars are not needed (many applications thus do not display them). As shown in figure 4.7, Clock does not have scroll bars. Because you can see only one thing inside the window—a clock—you have no need to scroll its window. Notice, however, that the Clock window has all the other window components.

The scroll bar along the bottom shifts the view across the document; the scroll bar along the right side moves up and down through the document. If the document is too large in one direction, only one set of scroll bars appears. A word-processing document, for example, may be too long to be displayed in a single view, so the scroll bars on the right side appear. If the document is narrow enough to fit in the window, however, the bottom scroll bars may not appear. Figure 4.8 shows a long list within a Notepad window.

Figure 4.7

Clock's display does not require scroll bars.

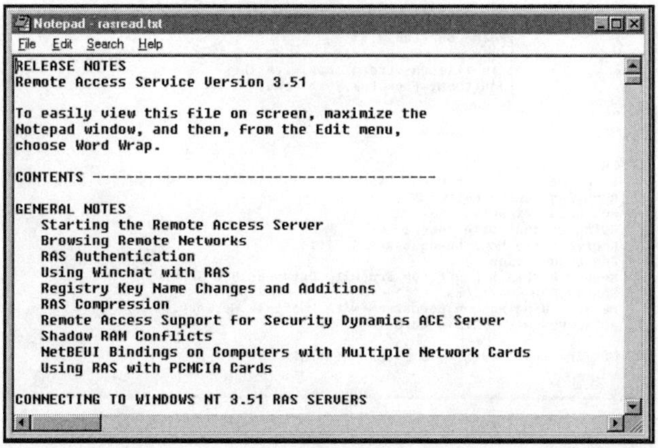

Figure 4.8

Notepad always displays scroll bars.

The *scroll buttons* are used to move the document view in the indicated direction. By clicking on the scroll button at the bottom of the scroll bar, you move the view down through the document. You can make the view scroll down (or up) the document by pointing to the scroll button and holding down the mouse button.

To move quickly through the document, you also can drag the *scroll box* along the scroll bar. If you know that the text you are looking for is two-thirds of the way down your document, for example, you can drag the scroll box to a position two-thirds down the scroll bar. When you release the mouse button, the view jumps to the new location.

Note Besides the scroll bars, most applications allow you to scroll document windows by using the Page Up and Page Down keys.

You can move the view down the document to display the next full window of information by clicking in the scrolling region below the scroll box. Or, by clicking above the scroll box, you move the view up one full window. This technique is recommended for reading through a document. Most programs move slightly less than a full window to enable you to recognize the transition between images.

The Control Menu

On the far left of the title bar is an icon of the application in the window. The icon functions as a button that activates the Control menu, which is a special menu that is a part of both icons and windows. You can click on the Control menu button of a Windows NT application to display the Control menu, as shown in figure 4.9.

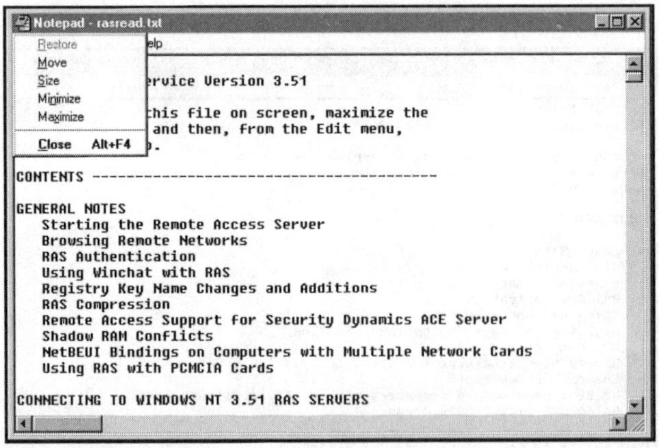

Figure 4.9

All Windows NT applications have the same items on the Control menu.

The same Control menu is displayed by clicking on a program icon on the Windows NT desktop. The Control menu is available even when an application is running full-screen. To display the Control menu for a maximized window, press Alt+spacebar or Alt+hyphen.

Note The Windows NT environment enables you to continue using your MS-DOS and POSIX-compliant Unix application programs. A DOS or POSIX application that runs under the Windows NT environment is said to run within a DOS or POSIX window.

Windows NT enables DOS programs to use graphics mode and text mode when running in a window. Most DOS and POSIX windows have the Control menu, as shown in figure 4.10.

Most of the commands on the Control menu are for tasks that can be performed by manipulating the window with the mouse. One of the requirements of the Windows NT user interface is that all tasks also can be performed by using the keyboard. The Control menu provides a way of moving, resizing, and controlling windows by using the keyboard. These commands appear on all Control menus (whether from an application, document, DOS, or POSIX window).

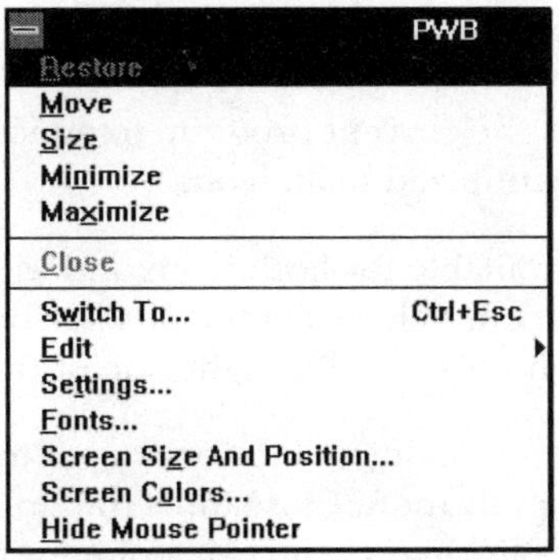

Figure 4.10

The Control menu.

- The **R**estore command is available in Control menus when an application is maximized or minimized. This command is used to return a window to the position and size it was before it was maximized to full-screen or minimized.
- The **M**ove command is active only when a window is not full-screen. When you choose it, the mouse pointer changes to a four-arrow pointer. By pressing an arrow key, you can move the current window. You can continue to use the arrow keys to move the window in small increments, or you can move the mouse. The window moves with the mouse without your having to press the mouse button; clicking (or pressing Esc) stops the window's movement and deselects the command. A window also can be moved by dragging the title bar to the new location. Press Enter to end the procedure.

Note Some actions are quicker to perform by using the keyboard. When you use a DOS program in a window and you want to switch to full-screen mode, for example, press Alt+Enter. To perform the same action by using the mouse, you must select the program's control button and choose the Ma**x**imize command.

- The **S**ize option is available only when a window is not full-screen. When you choose **S**ize, the pointer changes to a four-arrow mouse pointer (as with the **M**ove command). You can press any arrow key to select a border, and you then can extend or shrink that dimension of the window. If you press the right arrow once, for example, the right border is selected; if you press the right arrow again, the right border expands to enlarge the window. If you press the left arrow, however, the right border shrinks to reduce the window's size.

Note You also can select a corner by first selecting one side and then using the arrow to select one of the adjacent sides. You now can expand the window in two directions. Press Enter to end the procedure.

- The Mi**n**imize option shrinks the current program to an icon; it is not available when a program already is minimized to an icon.
- The Ma**x**imize command is available for both icons and windows, enlarging the current window to fill the screen. (These commands perform the same tasks as the minimize and maximize buttons on the right side of the menu bar.)
- The **C**lose option is used to close a document window or to quit a program. If the Control menu is for an application, **C**lose quits the program. The same task can be performed by double-clicking on the Control menu button. If you forget to save the contents of a document window before you choose **C**lose, Windows NT asks whether you want to save the document before closing.
- Clicking on the Run option displays the Run window, which allows you to display the Clipboard or the Control Panel.

The following exercise takes you through some of the options in a Control menu:

1. Select the Notepad window, then choose the Control menu.
2. Choose **M**ove. The pointer changes to a four-way arrow.

Note Move is grayed out if the window it is in is maximized—there is nowhere to move such a window.

3. Press the right-arrow key on the keyboard a few times.
4. Press Esc.
5. Press Alt+spacebar to open the Control menu again.
6. Choose Mi**n**imize. Notepad minimizes to an icon on the Taskbar.
7. Click on the Notepad icon in the task bar with the secondary mouse button. The Control Menu displays.
8. Choose **R**estore. Notepad restores to a window.

To help you understand the way other commands work in the Control menu, experiment with them. When you are ready to go on, the next section shows you the other types of menus available in a Windows NT program.

Menus

Every Windows NT program, even a simple application such as Clock, has a menu bar. The *menu bar,* which always is located directly below the title bar, has a collection of the most commonly used commands. The menus within the Windows NT environment are drop-down menus. By selecting a menu name from the menu bar, you can view a list of menu items that drop down from the menu bar. The menu bars of Word for Windows are shown in figure 4.11.

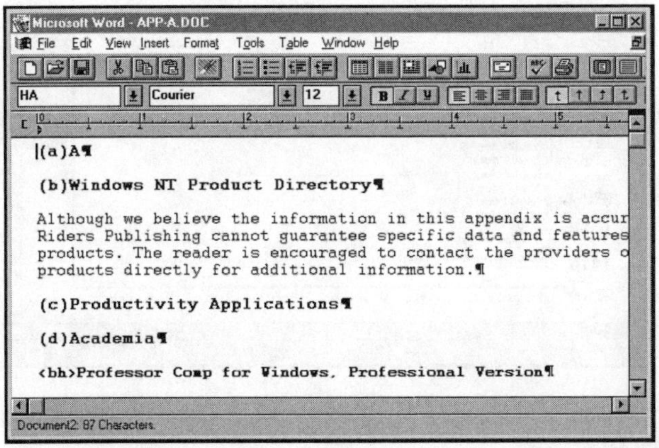

Figure 4.11

Menu bars for Word for Windows.

The menu system in Windows NT is very different from that of older DOS and Unix programs. Windows NT's menus and dialog boxes (discussed later) have streamlined the way you interact with programs. A Windows NT menu is designed to tell you which options are available at any level of the Windows NT menu system.

All menus in a Windows NT application appear as names on the menu bar. Whenever possible, the commands and their locations on the menu bar are consistent from program to program. File, for example, always is the first menu choice, and Help always is the last. The Open command always is on the File menu, and it is used by most programs to open their data files. These common menus are described in the next section.

Common Menus

The File, Edit, and Help menus typically are consistent from one program to another. This consistency is a powerful time-saver for you when you learn a new Windows NT program. After you learn to exit one Windows NT application, for instance, you know how to do it in every other Windows NT program. If you have ever opened a new MS-DOS or Unix program and not known how to quit the program (without finding the computer's on/off switch), you can appreciate a consistent method for such routine operations as quitting applications and opening, saving, and printing documents.

The File Menu

Several commands nearly always are found on the File menu. The last command on the File menu, for example, typically is Exit, and the first three File commands usually are New, Open, and Close. More important, the dialog box generated by selecting the Open command also is similar from program to program. Figure 4.12 shows the Open dialog box from Word for Windows 95.

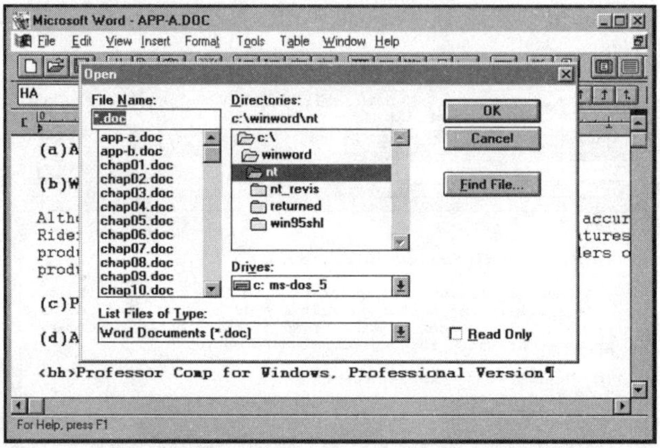

Figure 4.12

Open dialog box from Word for Windows.

The next pair of commands found on most File menus are those used to save a file—Save and Save As. Not only are the commands the same, but the accelerator keys and shortcut keys (if any) are the same between programs.

The other command commonly found on the menu is the Print command. Depending on the program, a single Print command or a collection of printing menu items (such as Print, Printer Setup, and Print Preview) can be found here.

The Edit Menu

The Edit menu contains commands for moving data between a program and the Windows NT Clipboard, which is a common storage area for data. Data is copied to the Clipboard, and then it is pasted from the Clipboard into the same program or a different program.

The Edit menu for most Windows NT programs contains the Undo, Cut, Copy, Paste, and Delete commands.

The Undo command enables you to cancel your last action; the remaining commands enable you to move data in and out of the Clipboard.

The Cut command removes the selected data (you must select the data prior to cutting it) from the program's window and places it in the Clipboard.

The Copy command copies selected data from the program to the Clipboard.

The Paste command pastes (copies) data from the Clipboard into the program's window.

The Delete command deletes selected data from the program's window, but it does not place the deleted data in the Clipboard.

Many Windows NT programs also contain other commands in their Edit menus. The Edit menu for WinGIF, for example, contains a variety of commands for editing a graphics image (see fig. 4.13).

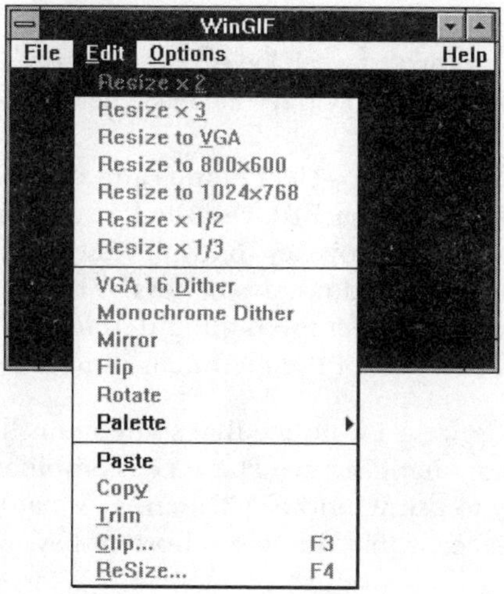

Figure 4.13
WinGIF's Edit menu.

Common Menu Actions

As you work with menus, you will find that there are common actions you can perform. These actions are discussed in the following sections.

Selection Methods

The menu system of Windows NT is powerful because of the number of methods it provides to select menu items. The most obvious selection method is to use the mouse. By clicking on a menu name on the menu bar, you display that menu. By clicking on an item in the menu, you activate that item (usually a command). By clicking on another part of the display, you cancel that menu selection. You can close the menu, but leave the menu bar selected, by pressing Esc when a menu appears.

Another way to choose a menu option is to point to the menu name, press the mouse button to display the menu, drag the pointer down the menu until the desired menu item is highlighted, and then release the mouse button. (This method is more familiar for Macintosh users, because this is the way menus work on the Macintosh. In Windows NT, however, you do not have to hold the mouse button down to keep the menu displayed.)

Windows NT menu names on the menu bar contain one underlined character that can be used to select that menu. These characters are referred to as *accelerator keys.* Press Alt (or, in some applications, F10) to activate the menu bar, and then press the letter associated with the desired menu to cause the menu to drop down. When the menu appears, select a command by entering the accelerator key associated with that command. The **F**ile menu, for example, can be activated by pressing Alt+F. When the **F**ile menu appears, press **O** to select the **O**pen command.

Note The menu bar is activated when the Alt key is pressed, not when it is released. Note that you do not have to wait to see the menu before you choose the next letter.

The arrow keys also can be used to select menus and menu items. The menu bar first must be activated by pressing Alt or F10. Use the left- and right-arrow keys to move between menus; use the down-arrow key to display the contents of a menu. After a menu appears, press the up- and down-arrow keys to highlight the menu item you want, and then press Enter to select the highlighted item. Press Esc to close an open menu or to cancel the activation of the menu bar if no menu is displayed.

In the menu shown in figure 4.14, notice that some items have keystroke combinations written after the command name. These key combinations are called *shortcut keys* and are an efficient way to use Windows NT menus. A major advantage of the standard Windows NT interface is that the same shortcut keys work in most Windows NT programs.

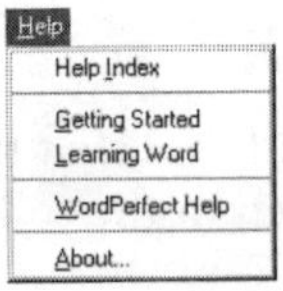

Figure 4.14
Many commands on the Edit menu are universal to Windows NT programs.

Because programs share a common interface, learning the shortcuts of the environment can save time. The command to copy information to the Clipboard is always the **C**opy command in the **E**dit menu (select the **E**dit menu, and choose the **C**opy command). You also can press Alt, **E**, and **C** at the same time. Or you can press Alt, and then press **C** after you press **E**.

An even faster way to invoke Copy is with the keyboard shortcut Ctrl+C (or Ctrl+Ins). These methods all work, regardless of your current program. The same process is followed in Excel and Word for Windows, for example.

Note Windows NT features two styles of keyboard shortcuts for cut, copy, and paste: the older Windows standard (Windows 3.0 and earlier) and the new standard for Windows NT/Windows 3.1. These are shown in the following table:

Function	Win 3.0	Win 3.1/NT 3.1 and later
Cut	Shift+Del	Ctrl+X
Copy	Ctrl+Ins	Ctrl+C
Paste	Shift+Ins	Ctrl+V

Menu items within Windows NT are more than a series of commands. Information on the menus changes to provide information about whether commands are available, which options currently are set, and which commands require multiple steps.

Dimmed Options

Windows NT is a "smart" operating environment; it knows, for example, that a maximized window simply cannot be made larger. One of the big advantages of Windows NT over MS-DOS and Unix programs is that you cannot select an option that is inappropriate or unavailable. Thus, if a menu item is unavailable, Windows NT automatically changes the color of the menu item to gray (by default). If you then try to choose the unavailable menu item, the program ignores your request.

Note Dimmed menu items sometimes are referred to as being grayed out.

Menu commands often are unavailable because you still need to select some object or because a previous action is required. The Undo command in the Edit menu, for example, is dimmed in all Windows NT programs until you do something that can be undone, such as deleting some text. You cannot cut or copy information from a document until data is selected; these options are dimmed until you make a selection. Likewise, because you cannot paste anything until something has been cut or copied, the Paste option is dimmed until information has been placed in the Clipboard.

The following exercise illustrates dimmed menus:

1. Select the Notepad window. Make sure that the README.TXT file is loaded on-screen.

2. Select **E**dit. Note that the **U**ndo, Cu**t**, **C**opy, and De**l**ete commands are dimmed.
3. Select **E**dit, and choose Select **A**ll. The entire document is highlighted.
4. Select **E**dit again. Note that the Cu**t**, **C**opy, and De**l**ete commands are no longer dimmed.
5. Choose the **C**opy command.
6. Select **E**dit. Note that the **P**aste command is no longer dimmed.
7. Press Esc to cancel the menu.

Throughout Windows NT programs, menu items are dimmed (and sometimes removed) if the command does not make sense for the worksheet or document being displayed.

Items with a Solid Arrow

Some applications have an additional level of menus. A solid arrow to the right of a menu item indicates that a second menu appears after you choose that item (see fig. 4.15). This type of menu is called a *cascading menu.*

Figure 4.15

An example of a cascading menu.

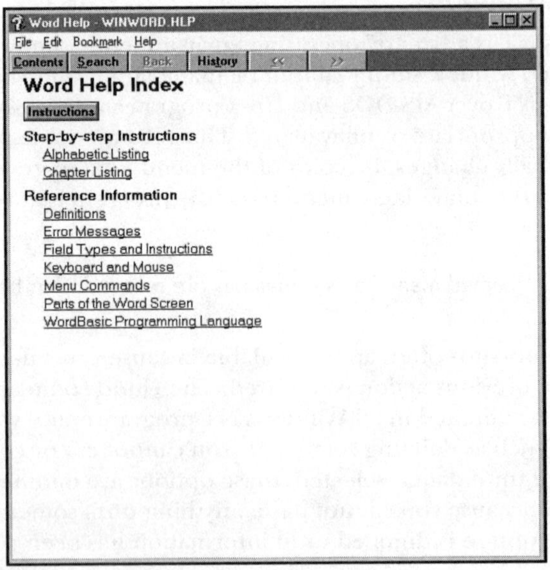

Cascading menus present a series of options or offer a new level of menu choices. If the menu presents a series of options, selecting the value sets the menu item equal to that value. If the cascading menu presents a series of menu items, choosing one of those items is the same as choosing an item from a first-level menu (a drop-down menu from the menu bar).

Items with Check Marks

In some programs, a menu-bar selection actually is a list of options that can be either on or off. If an option is turned on, it has a check mark beside it; if it is turned off, it is not checked. Figure 4.16 shows two checked options on the File Manager menu.

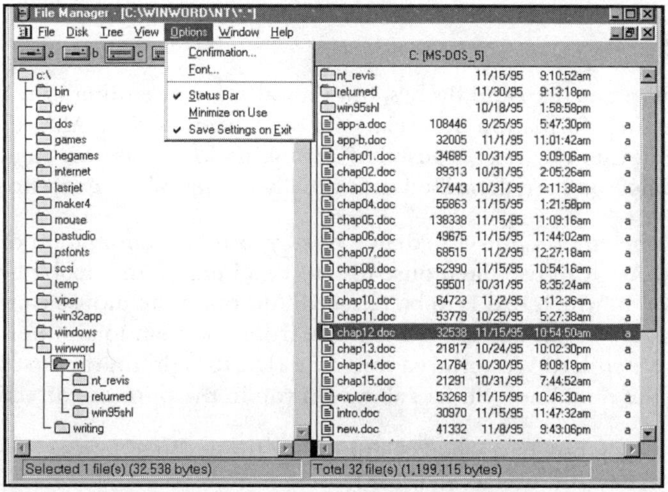

Figure 4.16
Active options within File Manager.

This type of menu item is referred to as a *toggle switch.* Just like a light switch, it can move between two settings. Some programs change the name of the item rather than display a check mark, but this method of handling a toggle switch has grown increasingly uncommon among applications.

Items with an Ellipsis

The *ellipsis* symbol (three periods) means "continued." An item on a Windows NT menu that is followed by an ellipsis is continued within a dialog box.

A *dialog box* is used within Windows NT to obtain additional information from the user. When a menu item is followed by an ellipsis, additional information is needed to complete the command. When you choose **F**ind from the **S**earch menu in Notepad, for example, Windows NT produces a dialog box similar to the one in figure 4.17. This dialog box asks what you want to search for and how you want to search for it.

The ellipsis provides guidance when you explore a new program and are not sure what is safe to click on. If the menu option has an ellipsis, you can safely click on it and review the box that pops up on-screen without activating any commands. You can press Esc to cancel the dialog box without making any changes.

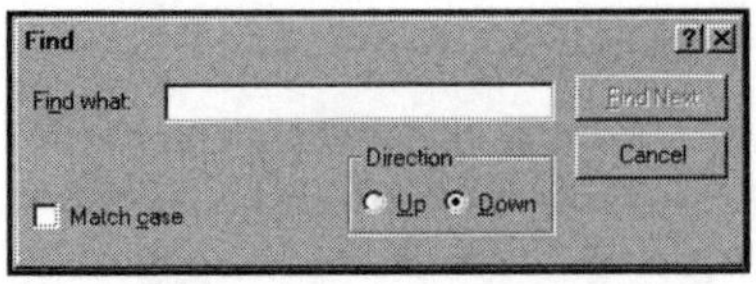

Figure 4.17
Notepad's Find dialog box.

Dialog Boxes

Dialog boxes come in many sizes and flavors, but they all have one thing in common: they gather and contain information that relates to the current action. Although each dialog box is different, they all are composed of a combination of specific items. The controls used in a dialog box are described individually in the following sections.

The information can be entered into the dialog box by using a combination of the mouse and keyboard. You can use the mouse to select an item on the dialog box, including the location in which text is to be entered. Although the mouse can be used to directly select any item, Tab is used to move from one item to another, in a pattern similar to the standard Western reading style (left to right on the first line, and then moving to the next line). Shift+Tab moves you in the opposite direction.

Most items within a dialog box have an accelerator key (underlined letter). To select the item, press the Alt key and the accelerator key.

Text Boxes

A *text box* (sometimes referred to as an *edit box*) is a rectangular box that accepts input from the keyboard. The simplest way to use a text box is to start typing. In most text boxes, any existing text is highlighted automatically and is deleted when you begin typing.

You also can use the mouse (or the arrow keys) to move to a specific point within the text and insert new text. Backspace and Del can remove single characters or blocks of characters when highlighted with the mouse.

Note To highlight with the keyboard, move to the starting location, hold down Shift, and use the arrow keys to move to the ending location.

Some text boxes, such as the Annotate dialog box shown in figure 4.18, accept multiple lines of text. To start a new line in this type of text box, use Ctrl+Enter. To start a new paragraph (skip a line), press Enter (Shift+Enter also works to maintain compatibility with other versions of Windows). Multiple-line text boxes are taller than single-line boxes.

You can use the cut, copy, and paste shortcut keys in a text box.

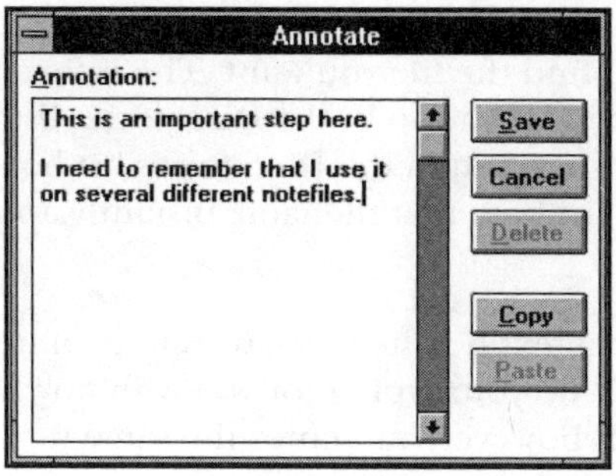

Figure 4.18

The Annotate dialog box.

List Boxes

A *list box* shows choices, often sorted alphabetically. You can scroll up and down the list by using vertical scroll bars such as those used to navigate a window's screen display. When the desired item is displayed anywhere in the list box, you can select it with the mouse by clicking on it. If you double-click on an item in the list, the program selects the item and closes the dialog box.

If you do not use a mouse, you can move to the list box (either by using Alt and the accelerator key, or by pressing Tab), and then press the up- and down-arrow keys to make your selection. When the selection has the gray outline, press the spacebar to highlight it, or press Enter to select the item and close the dialog box in a single step. You also can use Page Up and Page Down to move through the list more quickly.

Although most list boxes enable you to select only a single item, some enable you to select multiple items from a single list. To select multiple items with the mouse, hold down Shift while you click on additional items. If you use the keyboard, hold down Ctrl, move the focus with the arrow keys, and press the spacebar for each item you want to add. This type of list box is common in programs that manipulate groups of files, such as the File Manager.

Most list boxes that are sorted also support a technique known as *First Character Goto.* In Excel's Functions list under the Paste Function command on the Formula menu, hundreds of items are available. If you want to select the WEEKDAY function, for example, you must scan more than 100 choices before WEEKDAY scrolls into view. With the First Character Goto technique, press **W**; you are taken to the first entry that begins with the letter W in the list.

Some list boxes and text boxes are linked to form a unit known as a *combination box,* such as the File Name text box and the list box in the File Open dialog box (refer to fig. 4.12).

You can access a file by typing its name directly in the text box or by scrolling through the **F**ile Name list box until you find the file you want. The information displayed in the files list box is based on the value shown in the **D**irectories list box (it displays the files contained in the directory specified in the **D**irectories list box). After you choose a filename from the **F**ile Name list box, that filename instantly appears in the text box.

When a list box is connected to a text box like this, selecting an item from the list is the same as having Windows NT do your typing for you with no chance of error. You can elect to do your own typing, however, and enter the same information into the text box directly from the keyboard.

Drop-Down Lists

A normal list box takes up a large amount of space inside a dialog box. In the Files list box in the Open dialog box in the File menu, for example, room for eight filenames exists. A drop-down list is a space-efficient way of combining a text box and a list box, enabling several lists to be included in a single dialog box, as shown in figure 4.19.

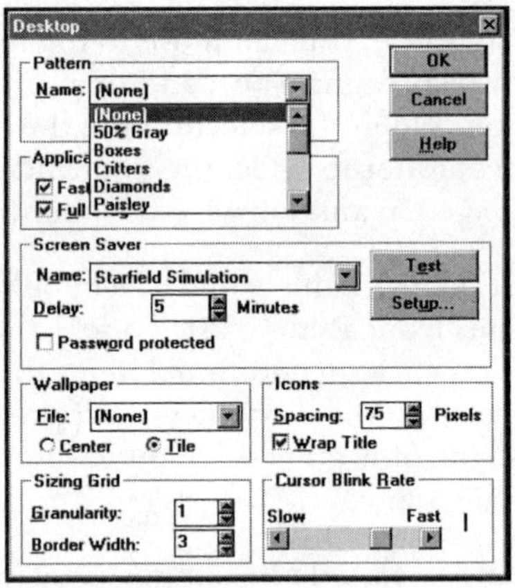

Figure 4.19
Drop-down lists in the Desktop dialog box.

Note To display the drop-down list in figure 4.19, open the Control Panel (double-click on the Control Panel icon). Select Desktop by double-clicking on it. The **N**ame text box in the Pattern box is a drop-down list.

The text box displays the most current selection from the list (or the top item, if no item was selected previously), and it has a pull-down button on the right side. (The *pull-down button* looks like other buttons, but it contains a down arrow.) You can click on the pull-down button to display the other choices available for that item. You then can make your selection as you would in any list box.

For keyboard use, move to the drop-down list by pressing Tab or pressing Alt, followed by the character associated with the drop-down list box. The icon on the drop-down list is an underlined down arrow. The items on the list can be displayed by pressing Alt and the down arrow.

When the list appears, you can press a letter to take you to that portion of the list. If you type **C**, for instance, the highlight bar instantly moves to Critters in the selection list. This is another example of the First Character Goto feature, discussed as part of the standard list box. Finally, if you highlight the text in the top portion of the drop-down list, you can enter text directly as though it were a standard text box.

Tabs

When you use menu items to open child windows, one window often gets lost in the background. Finding hidden windows often requires that you either iconify or move visible windows.

An alternative to layering window upon window is the use of tabs. Tabs are similar to the tabs on file folders. When you look in a file drawer full of file folders, you can pick out the folder you want by looking at the tabs on top of the folders where the name of the folder is written. Tabs in Windows NT work the same way. Although many windows in a tab display are, in effect, on top of one another, you have easy access to any of them by clicking on their tab, which is always visible. Figure 4.20 shows you an example of a tab in Windows NT.

Figure 4.20
Using tabs in windows.

Notice that all of the tabs remain visible, regardless of which window is on top.

Option Buttons

Option buttons (known in early versions of Windows as *radio buttons*) in a dialog box always are grouped so that only one button in each group can be selected at a time. (When you select a button in a group, any other button that was selected is turned off.) Option buttons are referred to as radio buttons because they resemble the tuning knobs of an old-fashioned radio.

Select an option button by clicking on it with the mouse, or by changing the focus to that group and using the arrow keys on the keyboard to select a particular button. Option buttons sometimes have underlined shortcut keys in their description labels; they can be selected by holding down Alt and pressing the underlined letter key.

The paper Orientation group on the Document Properties dialog box, shown in figure 4.21, is an example of a group of option buttons. It contains two choices: **P**ortrait and **L**andscape orientation. The printer's paper can be in only one of these two conditions, so if you choose **L**andscape, the dialog box automatically turns off the **P**ortrait button.

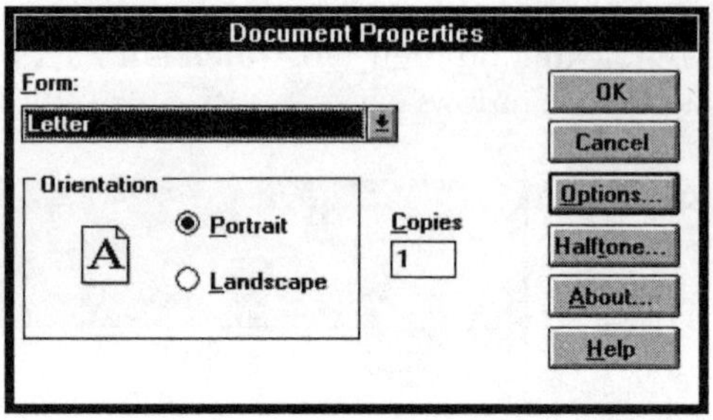

Figure 4.21

Only one choice in the Orientation group can be selected.

Option buttons are grouped within a named border, called a *group window.* (The option buttons discussed in the Printer Setup dialog box are in the Orientation group.) Option buttons within a group are mutually exclusive: if you select one, all others are deselected.

Check Boxes

A *check box* enables you to specify a preference in the same way you check a box on an order form. When the box is checked, it is considered on or true; when it is empty, it is considered off or false. The Word for Windows Print Options dialog box, shown in figure 4.22, for example, has several check box items, including **D**raft Output, **R**everse Print Order, and **U**pdate Fields. You also can include **S**ummary Info, **F**ield Codes, **A**nnotations, and **H**idden Text.

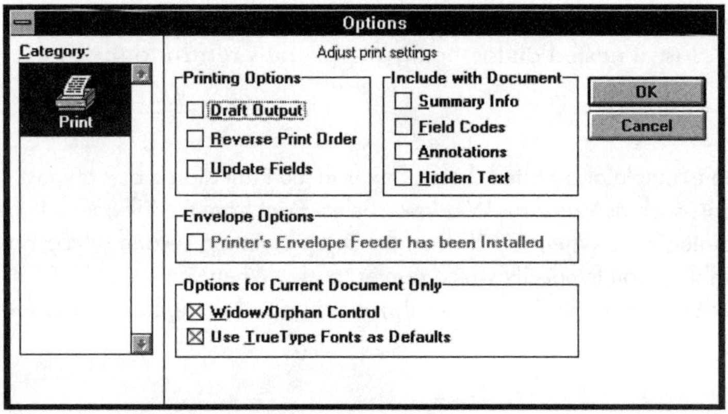

Figure 4.22
Any combination of check boxes can be selected.

A check box acts like a toggle switch: clicking on an empty box checks it, and clicking on a checked box clears it. Most check boxes can be accessed by using an accelerator key.

If you use the keyboard, press the spacebar to change the status of a check box from checked to cleared (or from cleared to checked). Check boxes are grouped by the type of action they control, but, unlike option buttons, the grouping is not restrictive: each check box is independent of the other check boxes within the group. You can select one, none, all, or any combination of check boxes within any dialog box.

Command Buttons

The command buttons on a dialog box are used after you complete all necessary information. Two command buttons included on almost every dialog box are OK and Cancel. By clicking on OK, you tell Windows NT to proceed with your selections; clicking on Cancel tells Windows NT that you want to exit without selecting.

The keyboard equivalent of Cancel is always Esc. Enter is a key equivalent for the default command button. (The *default* is the item selected before you make any changes.) In most dialog boxes, the OK button is the default; pressing Enter accepts the changes.

When you use the keyboard and move to a command button, the outer edge of the button becomes darker, meaning that the button is selected. You will notice that the OK button in figure 4.21 is selected, whereas the Cancel button is not. You can activate the current button by pressing Enter.

Besides OK and Cancel buttons, another type of button opens a second dialog box on top of the existing one; this *nested dialog box* typically contains related information that cannot fit on the first dialog box or that rarely needs to be changed. (Such a button invariably will be labeled with ellipsis dots to indicate that another dialog box will appear.) When you close a nested dialog box, you generally return to the first-level dialog box.

Note A common example of a nested dialog box is in the Print dialog box of most applications, such as Word for Windows. Select **P**rint from the **F**ile menu to open the Print dialog box. When you click on the **S**etup button, a second dialog box opens, enabling you to specify which printer to use. When you close the Print Setup dialog box by clicking on OK or Cancel, you return to the original Print dialog box.

Icons

Windows NT Explorer, like Windows 95, uses *icons* on the Taskbar to represent active applications. When you start an application, it appears in a window on top of the Root window. At the same time the window displays, the application's icon appears on the Taskbar.

When a window is displayed, the icon on the Taskbar associated with it appears to be pushed down. When a window is minimized, by pushing the dash button on the right side of the Title bar, the icon looks like a button that is raised.

In Windows NT 3.*x*, when you minimized an application, it shrank to an icon at the bottom of the screen. In Windows NT Explorer, when you minimize an application, it disappears from the Root window. All that is left is its icon on the Taskbar.

An icon is a representation of an application or device. Within Windows NT, an icon is a small picture (usually 32×32 screen dots) that represents an application, a file, or an action. Icons can be manipulated by the mouse by clicking on it with the primary mouse button to restore its window, or by clicking on it with the secondary mouse button to display the icon menu. The icon menu has the same options as the Control menu, which was previously described.

Application programs that are minimized to icons still run, and they can perform complex actions. They do not occupy as much memory, however, because they do not need to display their application window. (They often run in the background.) An application shrunk to an icon also presents less clutter on the desktop than if it is left as an application window.

Application Shortcuts

Application Shortcuts are links to application executables. The Shortcut appears as an icon on the Root window. When you double-click on a Shortcut, its application starts. The difference between icons and Shortcuts is that an icon appears on the Taskbar only when its application is running. A Shortcut appears on the Root window whether its application is running or not.

Using Shortcuts

New in Windows NT is the opportunity for you to store any application as an icon on the Root window. Instead of having to display the Programs to access application icons in version 3.*x*, application icons, called Shortcuts, can be accessed directly. Double-clicking on a Shortcut invokes its application.

Note In terms of technical jargon, a Shortcut is really a link. A Shortcut is not a program; it merely represents a program. If you delete a Shortcut, for example, you delete only the reference to the program, not the program itself.

The following example shows you how to create a Shortcut for the clock, but you can use the same procedure for making a Shortcut for any application.

1. Click on the Start button and then click on the Programs option in the Start button menu. In the submenu, click on the Accessories option.
2. Click on the Clock. The clock displays.
3. Click on the Root window with the secondary mouse button to display the Root menu. Place the mouse cursor on the New option in the Root menu and then select Shortcut.
4. In the Shortcut box, browse in the Windows directory to locate the clock executable.
5. Click on Next in the Shortcut box and then the Finish button in the confirmation box. The Clock icon then appears on the Root window.

Application Groups

Application Groups are groups of icons that appear in the Programs menu (under the Start button's menu) and represent application groups. In Windows NT 3.*x*, you arranged icons in application groups in the Programs.

For example, when you installed a Windows application, very often the last action of the install program was to create an application group for the application in the Programs. The application group contained an icon of all of the application executables—including, for example, a readme file, the application itself, and a secondary application, such as a reference manual.

If you carry your CONFIG.SYS and AUTOEXEC.BAT files from Windows 3.*x* or Windows NT 3.*x* forward in to the latest version of Windows, the application groups appear in Explorer in the following way. When you click with the primary mouse button on the Start button, Explorer displays a menu of your application groups names, as shown in figure 4.23.

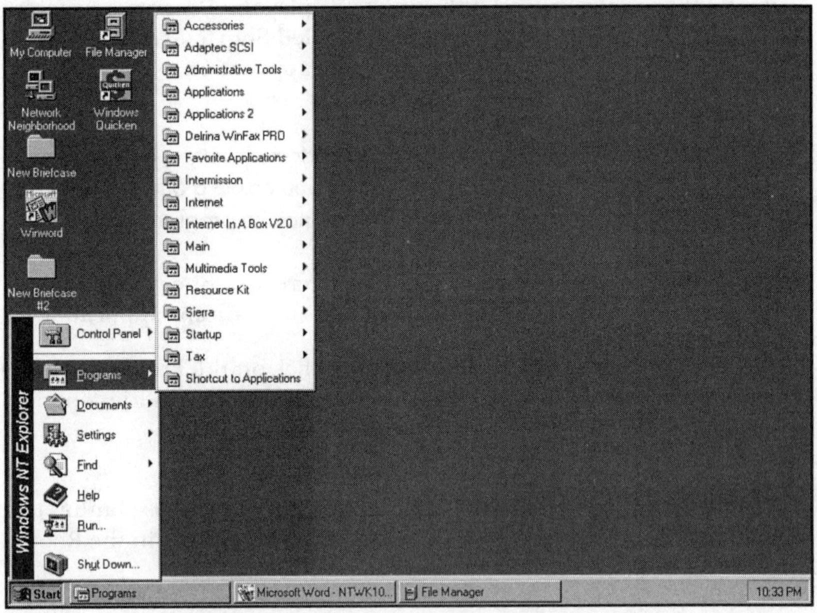

Figure 4.23
The Start Menu.

When you click on one of the application group names, another menu displays showing the names of the applications in the application group. Clicking on one of the applications starts the application.

Performing Common Windows Tasks

As mentioned earlier in the chapter, Windows NT applications and Windows NT itself follow strict guidelines regarding the design of the interface of an application.

Note

The reason for these guidelines is obvious. In the DOS world, time spent learning the command structure of one application, such as WordPerfect, does not help you when you learn another application, such as Lotus 1-2-3. Most DOS applications have unique command structures, so the steps required to open a file in WordPerfect are entirely different from those required by Lotus 1-2-3.

In contrast, Windows applications adhere to stricter command structure guidelines known as the *Common User Access* (CUA) standard. The benefit for the user is that after you learn a single Windows application, learning future applications becomes much easier because the basic commands are identical across applications. Therefore, you do not have to worry about whether to use Alt+F or Ctrl+F to open a file because all applications use a single menu action or key sequence. Additionally, you do not need to wonder where the print commands are hidden on the menu, because CUA helps ensure that the **P**rint command is always in the same place.

Windows NT's implementation of the CUA standard makes working with your PC and your programs easier. You can focus on the work at hand and not on figuring out how to use the software.

Basic File Operations

If a Windows NT application works with files, it presents a **F**ile menu as the first menu on the left side of the menu bar. All **F**ile menus in Windows NT applications are the same—they enable you to work with files by using the same command structure, no matter what the files contain. Every **F**ile menu enables you to perform at least four different file operations.

Creating a New File

In any Windows NT application, you can create a new, empty file by selecting the **F**ile menu and then choosing the **N**ew option (see fig. 4.24). The application opens a new, empty file and displays it in the workspace.

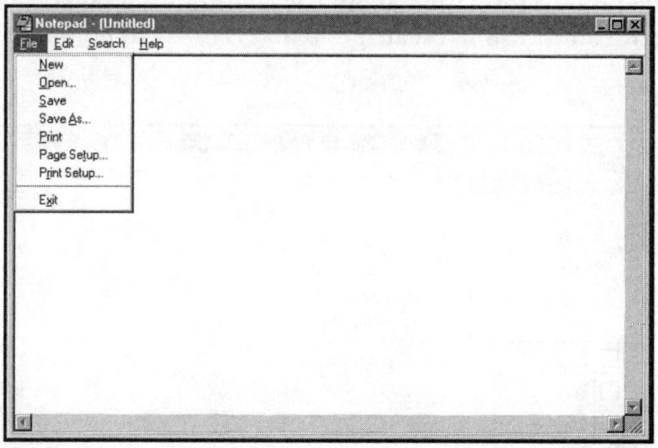

Figure 4.24

The File menu.

The Write and Cardfile applications provide examples of ways to use this action to create a variety of files in different applications. In Windows NT Write, the file you create has a format that keeps track of information about fonts, pictures, embedded objects, and text. Select the File menu and choose the New option to bring up a workspace that is ready to accept all information and display properly formatted text (see fig. 4.25).

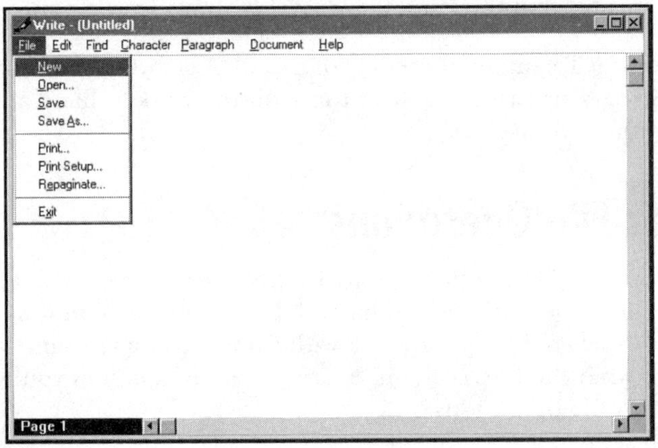

Figure 4.25

The New command in Write.

In Windows NT Cardfile, however, you choose the New command in the File menu to create a file that can contain graphical index cards, text, and pictures. The new file is presented as a single blank card in the workspace.

Windows NT Paintbrush presents a file in which you can turn individual pixels on or off. In addition, the file holds information about the color of each pixel. Select File, and then choose New in Paintbrush to create a file that is ready to hold information (see fig. 4.26).

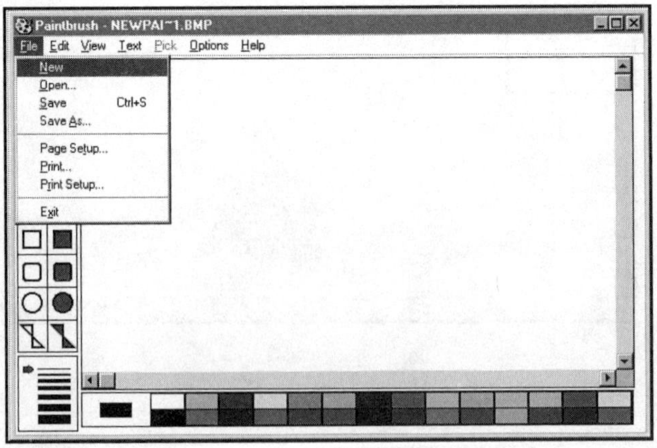

Figure 4.26

The New command in Paintbrush.

Opening an Existing File

Just as you can create new, empty files in different applications with the same command, you can open existing files in different applications by using the same command sequence.

In Windows NT applications, select the File menu and then choose the Open option. A dialog box appears for you to select the file you wish to open. After you respond, the application opens the requested file and displays it in the workspace.

The Write and Cardfile programs provide examples of ways the same command is implemented across applications that deal with very different data. When you select File and then Open in Write, for instance, a document appears in the workspace (see fig. 4.27).

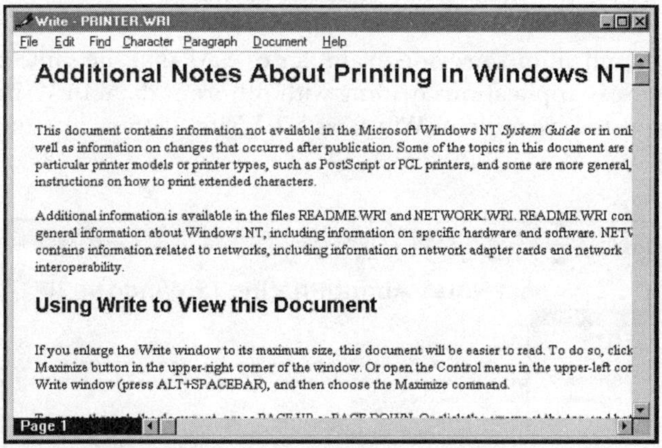

Figure 4.27

The result of the Open command in Write's File menu.

When you select File and then Open in Windows NT Cardfile, on the other hand, a set of index cards in the workspace appears (see fig. 4.28).

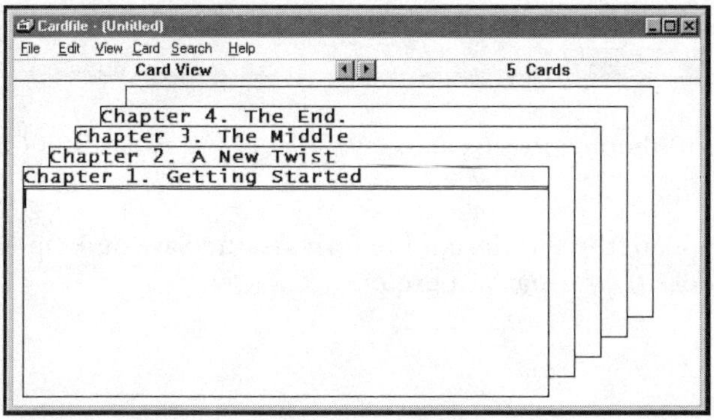

Figure 4.28

The result of the Open command in Cardfile's File menu.

Saving a File

Windows NT has the same command structure for saving files in different applications. To save a file, click on the **F**ile menu, and then choose **S**ave in any application. If you have not yet saved the file, a dialog box appears and asks you to type a file name into a text box. After you enter a file name, the application saves the file. If you have previously saved the file, the application saves the file under the same name. If you wish to save the file under a new file name, use the Save **A**s command (covered later in this section).

Note When saving a file, you usually do not need to type the extension, because most applications add their default file extension to your file name automatically (unless you have explicitly typed an alternative extension). Some applications, however, such as Quattro Pro for Windows, do not add an extension.

The Write and Cardfile applications provide examples of ways that the same command is implemented across applications dealing with different data. In Write, select **F**ile and then choose **S**ave to save a file in Windows NT Write file format (see fig. 4.29).

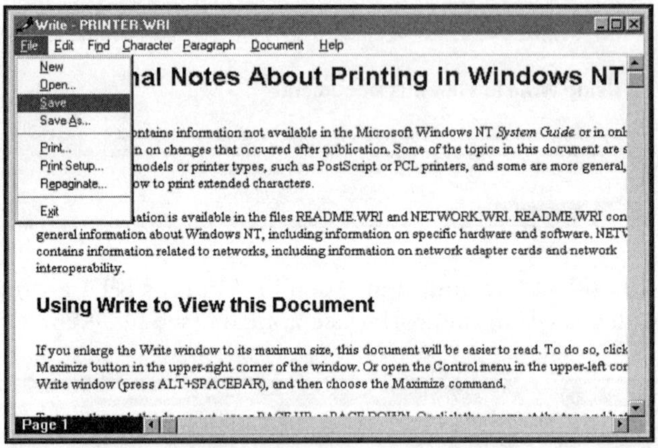

Figure 4.29

The Save command in Write.

In Cardfile, select **F**ile and then choose **S**ave to save a set of index cards in Cardfile's file format (see fig. 4.30).

Paintbrush can accommodate three different file formats; the Save and Open dialog boxes enable you to choose the format you prefer.

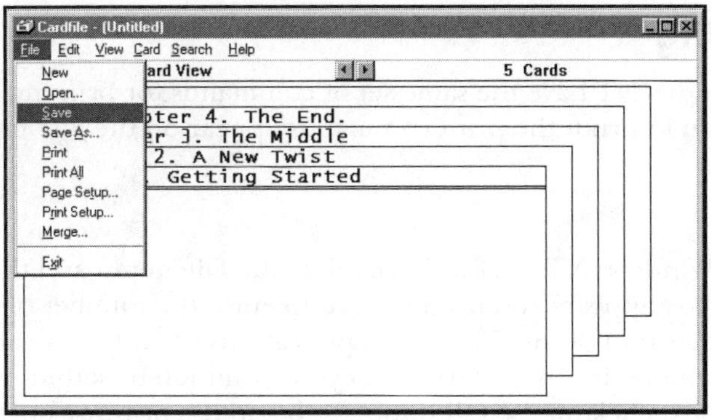

Figure 4.30

The Save command in Cardfile.

Note More programs are beginning to standardize shortcut key combinations to make life easier for Windows NT users. Shift+F12, for example, automatically invokes the **S**ave command in the **F**ile menu, whether you are in Word for Windows or Excel. As this trend continues, the investment of learning the standard Windows NT commands yields a greater and greater reward.

Saving a File with a New Name

In Windows NT applications, to save a file under a different name from the one with which you opened it, select the File menu and then choose Save As.

A dialog box appears (see fig. 4.31) and prompts you to type the new file name into a text box.

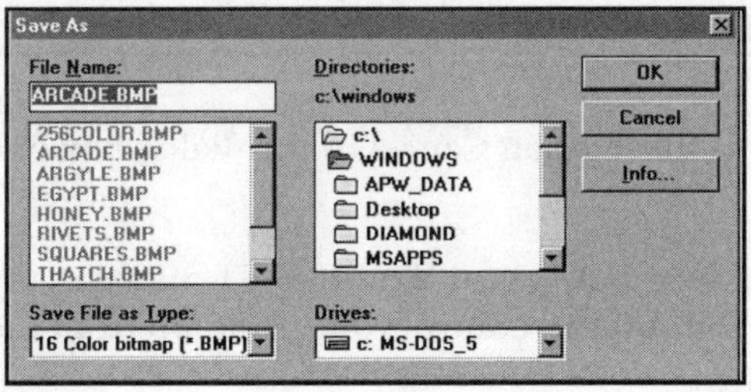

Figure 4.31

The Save As dialog box.

Usually you do not have to type the extension, because most applications add the default extension. After you respond to the Save As dialog box, the application saves the file.

Windows Printing

All applications in Windows NT have the same set of commands for printing files. If an application allows you to print, the print commands appear on the **F**ile menu.

Printing a File

To print a file in most Windows NT applications, select the **F**ile menu and then choose **P**rint. A dialog box appears and prompts you to enter the number of copies or to print only a selected portion of the file (some applications do not offer this option). After you determine the characteristics of your print job by setting the controls in this dialog box, click on the OK button to begin the printing operation.

After the print job begins, a dialog box appears to inform you that the file is printing (see fig. 4.32).

Figure 4.32

The Print Cancel dialog box in Write.

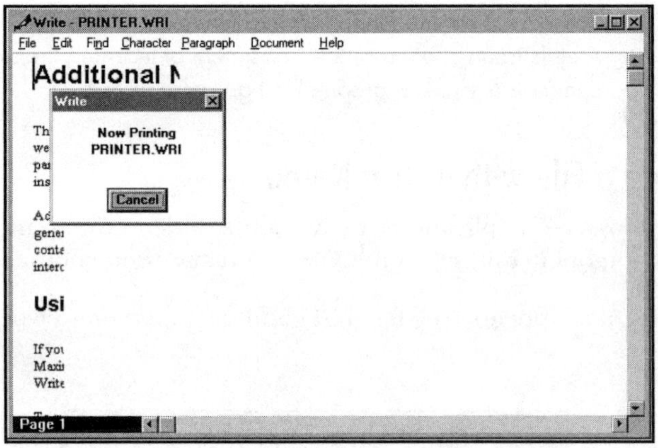

Halt the printing operation by clicking on Cancel in the dialog box or by pressing Esc.

After the Print Cancel dialog box disappears, Windows NT manages the print job, freeing you for other work. You still can control your print job from the Print Manager application if necessary.

Setting Up the Printer

Windows NT applications that enable you to print also enable you to control the printer setup. The actual management of the print job and communication with the printer is performed, not by individual applications, but by Windows NT itself. As part of this management, Windows NT gives application programs access to the installed printers.

You can access a Printer Setup dialog box and specify printer settings in each application. To access the printer setup, select the File menu and then choose the Print Setup option.

As figure 4.33 illustrates, the Print Setup dialog box contains a list of the printers attached to the system. Click on the name of the printer you want to use, and then click on the Setup button.

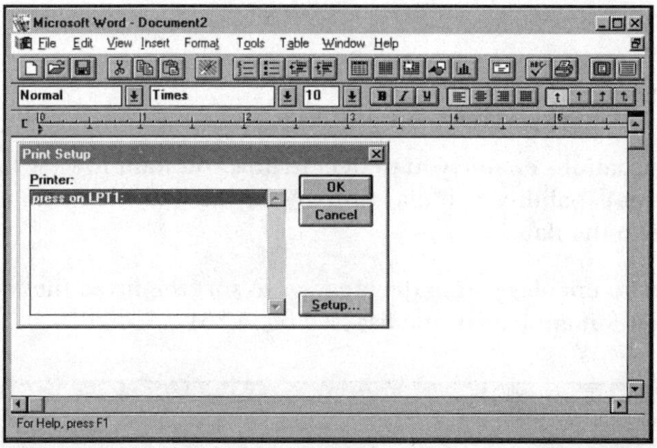

Figure 4.33

The Print Setup dialog box in Word.

Another dialog box then appears, which enables you to adjust the printer settings (see fig. 4.34). After you adjust the settings, click on the OK button. You return to the Printer Selection dialog box. Click on OK; your printer is set up.

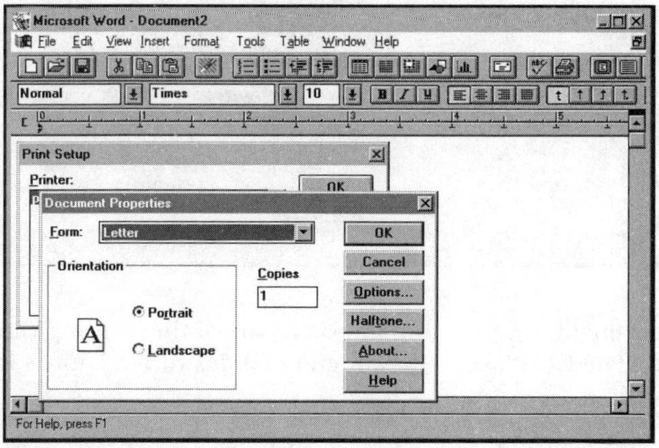

Figure 4.34

Document Properties dialog box.

Workspace Searches

Many Windows NT applications (particularly word processors and editors) enable you to search for information in their workspaces (refer to fig. 4.17).

Select the appropriate menu name to search for information in the application. A Search dialog box appears and asks you to enter the string to search for (you often are offered the opportunity to enter a replace string as well). Click on the Find button to begin the search.

Views of Your Workspace

Many Windows NT applications enable you to decide how you want to view the data. If the application has this capability, you may find a View menu, which enables you to display options specific to the data.

File Manager's View menu enables you to decide ways to sort the listed files and to select which file information appears in the list (see fig. 4.35).

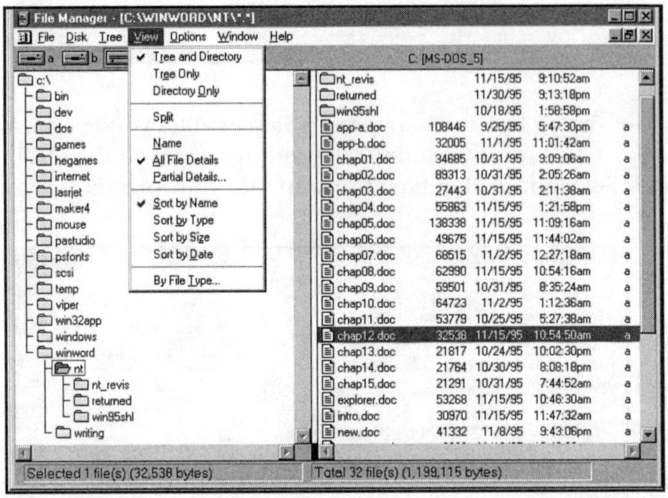

Figure 4.35

File Manager's View menu.

Paintbrush's View menu enables you to zoom in on a part of the drawing canvas or to zoom out of the canvas. The CD Player's View menu enables you to choose information about the current CD.

The View menu is less standardized across different Windows applications. Some applications do not provide the capability to change the view of your document or workspace; others place the command elsewhere. For example, Paradox for Windows enables you to change the view of a form or report through the Zoom option on the Properties menu.

Configuring Console Windows

Console windows are character-based and command-prompt windows. A new icon in the Controls Panel window, entitled Console, enables you to change console windows in the following ways:

- Specify the size of the cursor, screen buffer, and the position of the window.
- Enable or disable QuickEdit and Insert modes.
- Specify the background and text colors used in console windows and pop-up menus.
- Specify the font and point size of the type used in console windows and pop-up menus.

In earlier versions of Windows NT, you could change the same properties of console windows individually using the Properties command in the Control menu. (You display the Control menu by clicking on the dash button in the upper-left corner of a window.) The Console icon, however, allows you to change the properties of all Console windows at once.

Changing General Settings

When you open the Console Windows Properties window, you see four tabs with the General tab displayed by default. In this tab you can specify the settings for

- Cursor size
- Buffer size
- Window display size
- Enabling or disabling QuickEdit and Insert modes

To change the cursor size, use the following procedure:

1. Click on the Control Panel icon in the Main window.
2. Click on the Console icon. The Console Windows Properties window displays, as shown in figure 4.36.
3. To change the cursor size, click on the desired size in the Cursor Size portion of the window.

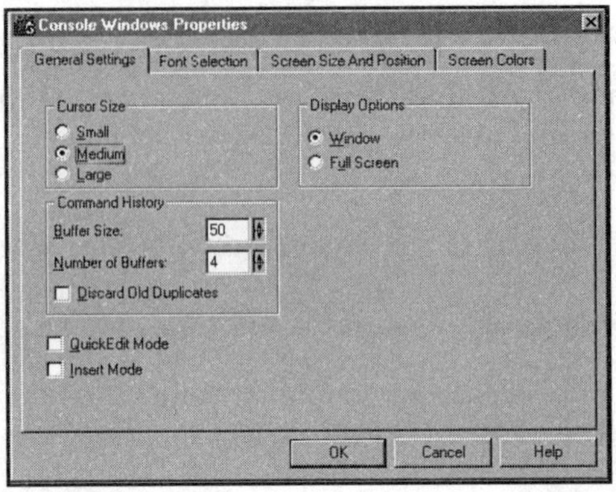

Figure 4.36

The Console Windows Properties window.

Changing the Command History Size

The Command History buffer records the most recent commands that you use. If you often use commands, you can use the Command History buffer to repeat the commands without retyping them. The default size of the buffer is 50 commands. You can change that size but, remember, the command buffer occupies memory. Setting it at too large a value can needlessly use memory.

You can also use the command buffer to store input for character-based programs that accept buffered input. (Software debuggers, for example, often use buffered input.) You can build a buffer for each program that accepts this kind of input. To do that, you must specify the number of buffers you want to create in the Number of Buffers field. Remember, however, that each buffer occupies memory.

You can display the command history in two ways:

- Press the F7 key and then use the up and down arrow to scroll through the list commands. When you find the command you want to reuse, press the Return key.
- Type part of the command and then press the F8 key as many times as you need until the command you desire is highlighted. Then press the Return key.

By default, the command history includes the last 50 commands you used regardless of whether or not you repeated commands. If you want to maximize the number of different commands stored in the command history, you can select the Discard Old Duplicates check box. This option removes from the command history any previous instances of a newly used command.

To specify the size of the Command History buffer, type the number of lines you want in the Buffer Size field in the Command History section of the General Settings tab.

Alternately, you can use the up and down arrows associated with the field to increment or decrement the number of commands the Command History buffer holds.

In the Number of Buffers field, type the number of character-based programs that can use buffered input. Alternately, you can use the up and down arrows associated with the field to increment or decrement the number of buffers to associate with character-based programs.

If you would like only one instance of a command in the Command History, click on the Discard Old Duplicates check box. Any time a command is added to the Command History, Windows NT eliminates any previous instance of the command in the Command History. Use this option to maximize the number of different commands that can occupy the Command History buffer.

Enabling QuickEdit and Insert Modes

Enabling QuickEdit allows you to save to a buffer characters highlighted in a document. You use this feature to cut and paste segments of a document without using the Edit menu.

To enable QuickEdit, click on the QuickEdit check box so that it is selected.

Enabling Insert mode enters characters that you type at the cursor. If Insert mode is not enabled, characters you type overwrite existing text.

Changing Display Options

Console panels can either display as a window or full screen. The default setting is window. If you wish to change the setting, however, you can click on the option you desire.

To change a the size of a Console window while it is displayed, type ALT+RETURN to toggle between settings.

RISC-based processors do not support full-screen mode, so the option does not appear to RISC users.

Changing the Default Size and Position of Console Windows

Windows NT allows you to specify the default position and size of Console windows by using the Screen Size and Position tab in the Console Windows Properties window, as shown in figure 4.37.

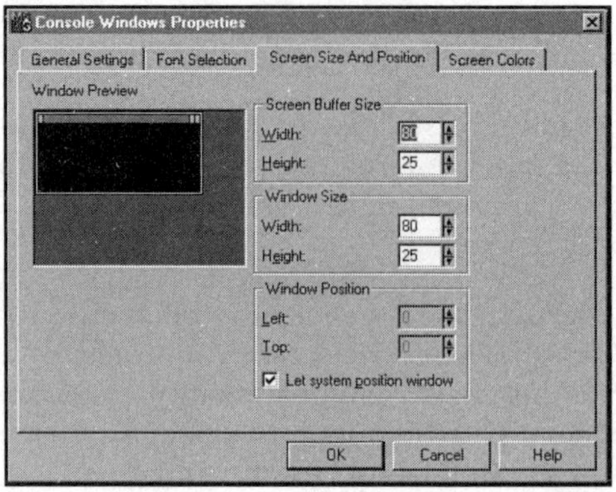

Figure 4.37

Screen Size and Position tab.

The Screen Buffer Size is the amount of memory, measured in the number of characters wide by the number of characters tall, allocated for each Console window. The Window Size, measured in the number of characters wide by the number of characters tall, is the amount of space taken up by the information on the window. You may not, for example, specify a larger Window Size than Screen Buffer Size. If, however, you specify a smaller Window Size than Screen Buffer Size, Windows NT adds a scroll bar to all console windows. Because a scroll bar is normally not needed with console windows, it is best to keep the Screen Buffer Size and the Windows Size the same.

You can either specify an absolute location on the screen to position all console windows, or you can let Windows NT place the windows directly on top of associated windows. You make that choice in the Windows Position section of the Console Windows Properties window.

To change the size and position of all console windows, use the following procedure:

1. Click on the Screen Size And Position tab in the Console Windows Properties window.

2. Type in the values for the height and width of the screen buffer in the Screen Buffer Size section. Alternately, use the up and down arrows to increment or decrement the screen buffer size, respectively.

3. Type in the values for the height and width of the window size in the Window Size section. Alternately, use the up and down arrows to increment or decrement the window size, respectively. Make sure the values are equal to or less than the values you used in step 2.

4. Choose the position of all console windows in the Window Position section:

- Click on the Let system position window check box to display console windows directly on top of associated windows.
- Type in the values for the left and top coordinates of the upper left corner of the Console window.

Alternately, use the up and down arrows to increment or decrement the coordinates, respectively.

5. Click on the OK button.

Specifying Screen Colors

The final tab in the Console Windows Properties window, Screen Colors, enables you to specify the color of the text and background of Console windows and pop-up windows that are associated with console windows. Pop-up windows are small windows that usually contain little more than text.

To change the colors used in console windows and their associated pop-up windows, use the following procedure:

1. Click on the Screen Colors tab in the Console Windows Properties window. Windows NT displays the Screen Colors tab, as shown in figure 4.38.

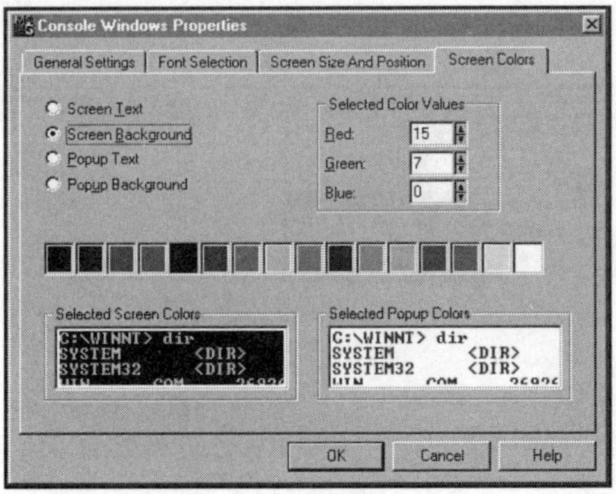

Figure 4.38

The Screen Colors tab.

2. Click on the Screen Text radio button.
3. Click on one of the colors displayed in the window. Notice that the color of the text displayed in the Selected Screen Colors section changes according to your color selection. Also notice that the Red, Green, and Blue values change according to your color selection in the Selected Color Values section.

4. Optionally, type in new values in the Red, Green, or Blue fields to change the color of the text. Alternately, use the up and down arrows to increment and decrement the color values, respectively.
5. Click on the Screen Background radio button.
6. Repeat steps 3 and 4 until you arrive at the color of background you like.
7. Click on the Pop-up Text radio button.
8. Repeat steps 3 and 4 until you arrive at the color of pop-up text you like. Notice that as you change the value of the colors of the pop-up text, the color text in the Selected Pop-up Colors changes accordingly.
9. Click on the Pop-up Background radio button.
10. Repeat steps 3 and 4 until you arrive at the color of background you like.
11. Click on the OK button.

Option Selection

Many Windows NT applications have special settings that you can use to customize appearance or behavior. An **O**ptions menu on the menu bar typically indicates this capability (see fig. 4.39).

Figure 4.39
The Options menu in Paintbrush.

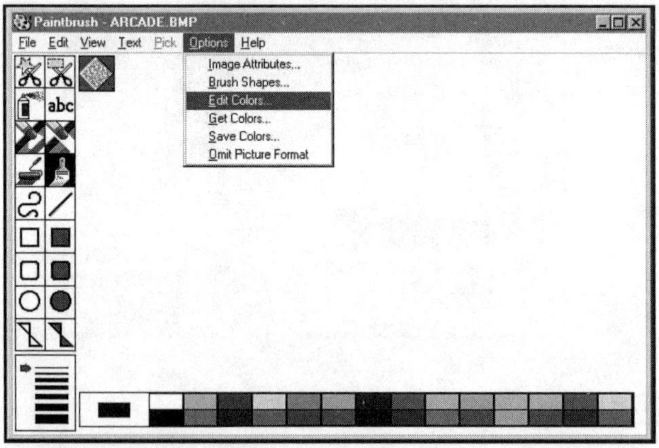

Note The Options menu is another case in which different application vendors have chosen different paths. Although many Microsoft products (such as Word for Windows and Excel) have an Options menu, Borland's Paradox for Windows provides a Properties menu to do essentially the same task.

Various applications enable different degrees of customization. Paintbrush, for instance, enables extensive control of its appearance and features.

File Programs, on the other hand, enables you to control only four aspects, which are found in the Options and Window menus. These are described as follows:

- If you select Auto Arrange, icons in a program group rearrange themselves after the program group is resized. The icons move into rows and columns that most efficiently use the available space.
- If you select Minimize on Use, icons shrink when you launch an application, clearing the screen of clutter and making all desktop space available to the application.
- The Save Settings on Exit option saves the position and status of the group windows when you end your Windows session.
- The Save Settings Now option enables you to save settings whenever you want.

Font Selection

Windows NT provides a pool of fonts that are available for each application for printing and displaying on-screen. You typically select a font within a given application by choosing a Font option from a menu.

Depending on the application, a dialog box might appear with a list of available fonts. Select the font you want by clicking on a font name. This font is used to write to the screen until you select another one. When you save the file, you save the current font. TrueType font files contain an unlimited number of font sizes because the fonts automatically are scaled to fit the screen.

Note Although TrueType renders virtually any point size for a given font, most applications display only those fonts with point sizes between 4–127 points.

You use different menus and commands to select fonts in different applications. The following four figures show different ways to select fonts in various applications.

Paintbrush presents a Text menu on which Fonts is an option (see fig. 4.40).

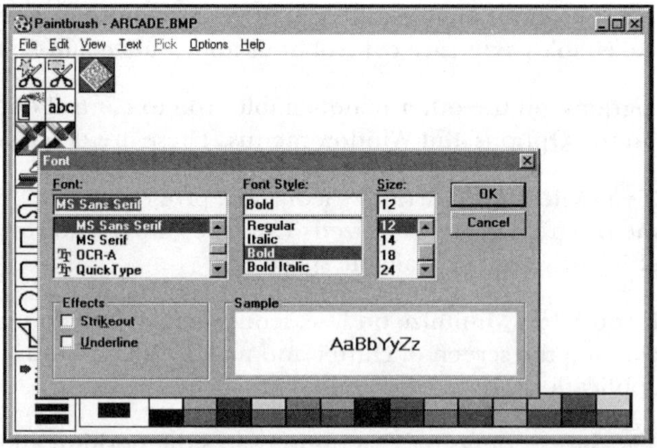

Figure 4.40

Font selection in Paintbrush.

Write presents a Character menu on which Fonts is an option (see fig. 4.41).

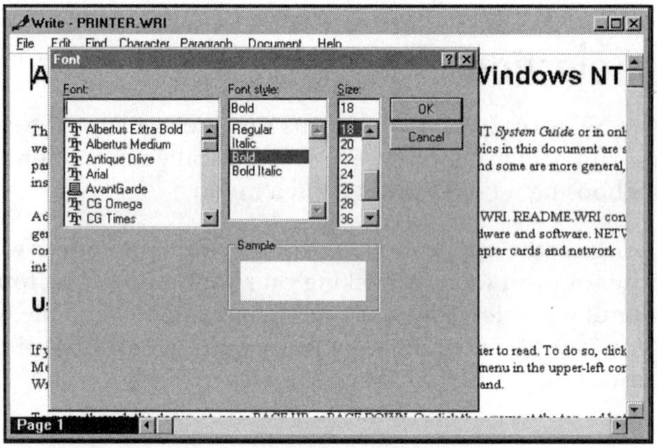

Figure 4.41

Font selection in Write.

Word for Windows uses two drop-down list boxes that enable you to select the font and its size (see fig. 4.42).

Microsoft Excel places the Font option on the Format menu.

Although applications use different ways to select fonts, Windows NT provides sophisticated fonts and font management for your applications. Because you do not have to install fonts for each separate application, you gain disk space and execution speed.

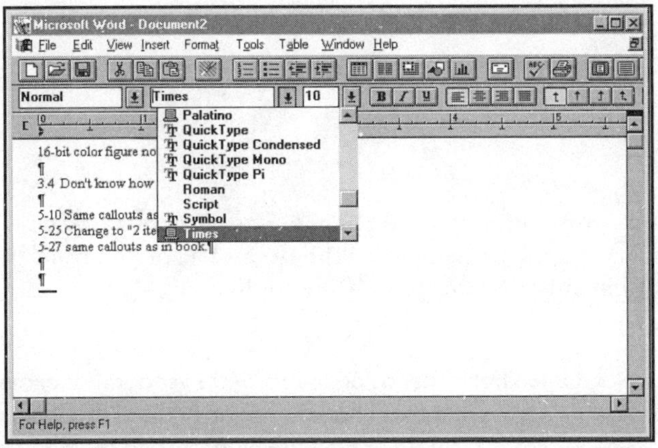

Figure 4.42

Font selection in Word for Windows.

Changing Font Settings

The Fonts tab, as shown in figure 4.43, enables you to choose the fonts and font size for all Console windows. Changing the size of the fonts makes the window size change correspondingly.

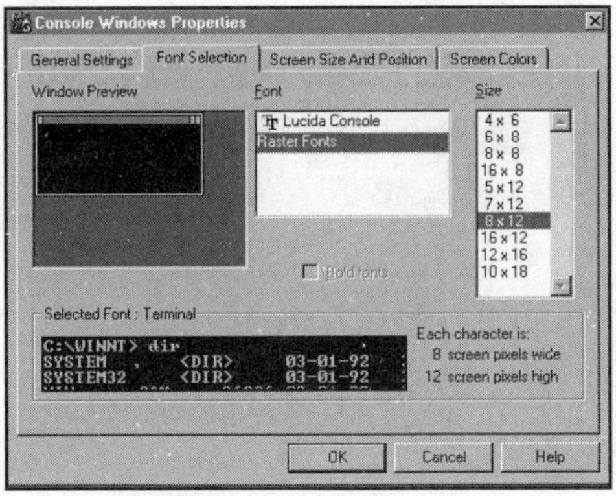

Figure 4.43

Fonts tab.

To change the fonts or font size, use the following procedure:

1. Click on the Font Selection tab. Windows NT displays the Font Selection tab.

2. Click on the desired font in the Font box.

3. Click on the desired font size in the Size box.

4. Look at the fonts displayed in the Selected Font:Terminal box. Change your font or font-size selections if necessary.

5. If you want bold fonts, click on the Bold fonts check box.

6. Click on the OK button.

Toolbars

Windows NT applications often offer you the chance to work with a *toolbar*, which is a strip of buttons that typically appears just under the menu bar of an application. You can initiate an action by clicking on a button on the toolbar.

Note The actual name of the toolbar depends on the software vendor. For example, Microsoft Word for Windows and Excel have toolbars, Borland Paradox for Windows and Quattro Pro for Windows have speed bars, and Lotus 1-2-3 and Ami Pro have SmartIcons. Although the names are different, they are designed to do essentially the same thing—speed up your work.

Every toolbar button has a picture that indicates its function. Normally, a button replaces several or many individual keystrokes or mouse actions. The **S**ave button on the Word for Windows toolbar (see fig. 4.44) is equivalent to the **S**ave option under the **F**ile menu.

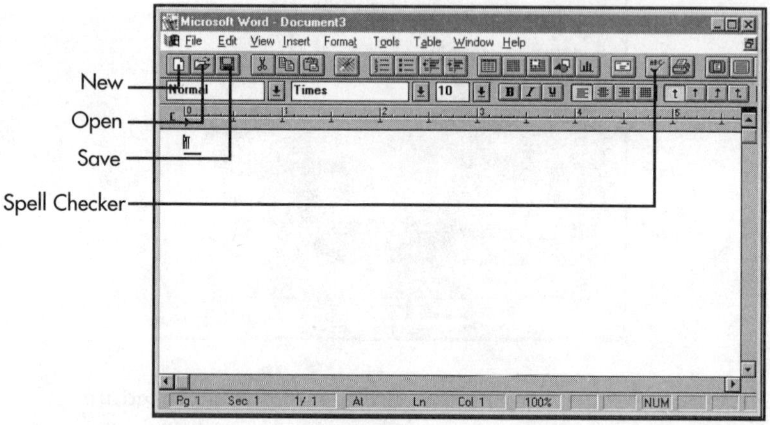

Figure 4.44

The Word for Windows toolbar.

Word for Windows uses a toolbar to provide immediate visual access to 22 common actions in the Word for Windows menu system, as you can see in figure 4.44. By clicking on the first button on the left, for example, you can create a new document. The next button opens an existing file.

Note Toolbars are gaining in popularity as the Windows interface becomes more complex. When Apple first introduced a menuing system in the Lisa and early Macs, the actual size of the screen was very small. As a result, using the mouse to select a menu option did not take too much hand movement.

With today's large 1024×768 super-VGA screens and complex menuing systems, selecting a toolbar option requires much less hand movement than the equivalent command found on the menu.

If you want to print, click on the Printer button. If you want to check spelling, click on the Spell checker button. You do not have to remember where the options are on the menus, so you are more efficient and less distracted by the Word for Windows command system.

A *toolbox* (see fig. 4.45) is similar to a toolbar. It presents a grid of tools represented by icons. Usually the grid has two columns. To select a tool, click on the corresponding icon in the toolbox. You then can use the tool to take an action in the workspace, such as spray painting in Paintbrush.

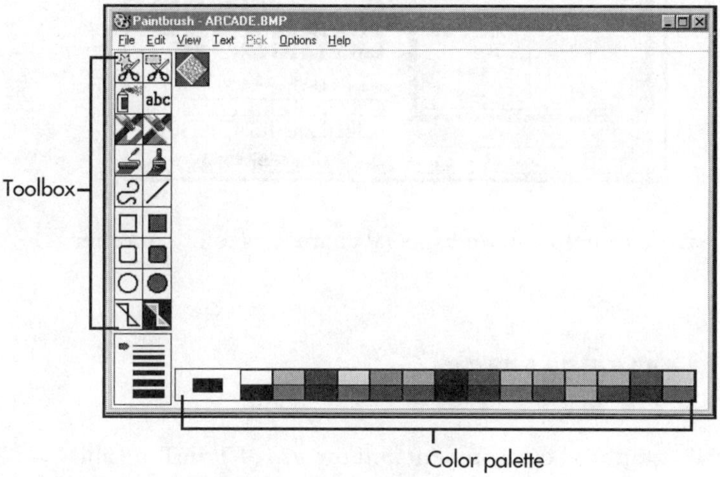

Figure 4.45

The Paintbrush toolbox.

The primary difference between a toolbar and a toolbox is the presence of command buttons with actions attached to them. Toolbars use buttons; toolboxes do not. Toolbar buttons initiate actions; toolbox icons select tools to use later. You find both kinds of tool-selection controls in Windows NT applications.

Palettes

A *palette* is similar to a toolbox, but it enables you to select colors. Paintbrush, for example, uses a color palette (refer to figure 4.45) to enable you to select the foreground and background colors as you draw.

To select a foreground color in Paintbrush, point to the color and click the left button. To select a background color, point to the color and click the right mouse button.

Other applications use palettes. Control Panel, for instance, uses one palette (see fig. 4.46) to enable you to select standard colors, and a separate palette to enable you to create and select custom colors. To see the color palette, activate the Control Panel and click on the Color Palette button.

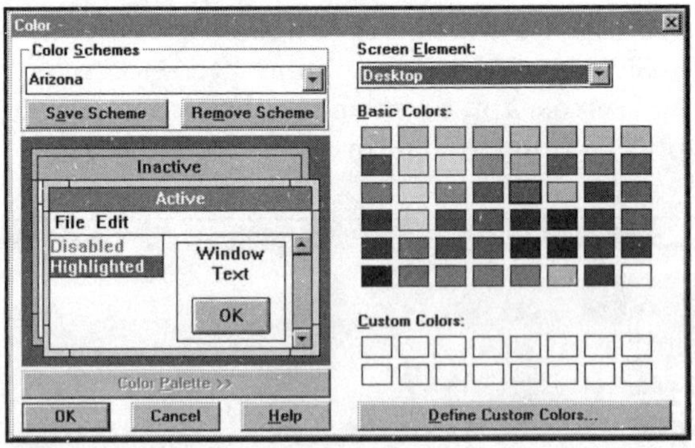

Figure 4.46
The Control Panel color palette.

Character Map uses a palette to help you find special characters to use in other applications.

Introducing WYSIWYG

Because of Windows NT's graphical environment and the use of TrueType and related technologies, Windows NT supports the principle of WYSIWYG. *WYSIWYG (What-You-See-Is-What-You-Get)* signifies that what you see on-screen in your application can be printed and look identical on the final output.

Most Windows NT applications can implement a WYSIWYG display because all their display elements are controlled by Windows NT rather than by the application itself. Windows NT renders all graphics and TrueType (and other scalable) fonts you use on-screen exactly as they will print on your printer. Figure 4.47 shows a WYSIWYG display.

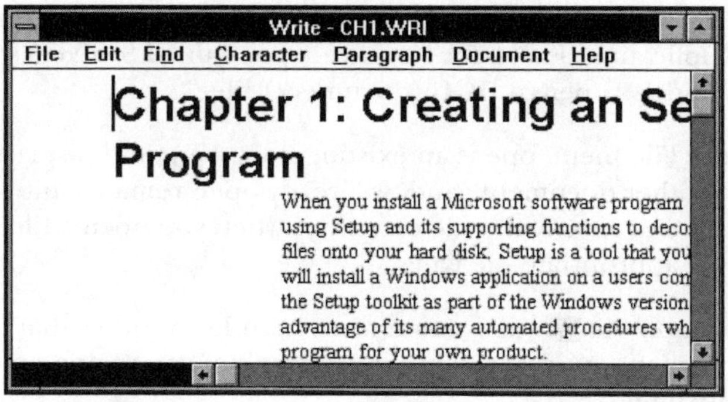

Figure 4.47
A WYSIWYG display in Write.

Note WYSIWYG depends on the types of fonts you are using. Bit-mapped fonts (such as MS Sans Serif and MS Serif) do not print exactly as they are viewed on-screen. In contrast, TrueType and ATM (Adobe Type Manager) fonts are WYSIWYG.

Managing the Multiple Document Interface

The Multiple Document Interface (MDI) is another standard to which Windows NT adheres. MDI enables you to open multiple files with a single application window, displaying each in a separate window called a *document window.* Because Windows NT document windows belong to the application window, they appear only in the workspace. Parts of a document window that slide past the workspace border are hidden from view.

MDI enables you to open multiple word processing documents and exchange data among them. You can open several Excel spreadsheets at once, for example, and link cells among them.

Note MDI offers simultaneous views of different drives or directory structures in File Manager.

MDI applications have a special menu, the **W**indow menu, for managing multiple documents in Windows NT. The **W**indow menu appears to the left of the **H**elp menu.

The **N**ew option on the **F**ile menu enables you to open a new document window.

You can enter data and save it in a file from this window. The type of file created by New depends on the application. Excel, for instance, opens an XLS (Excel spreadsheet) file; Word for Windows opens a DOC (document) file.

The **O**pen option on the **F**ile menu opens an existing document and displays it in an additional window. Any other document window already open remains undisturbed. Normally, you do not have to specify the file extension when you open a file. The application accesses only appropriate file types.

The **N**ew Window option on the **W**indow menu opens another window that displays the same file as the document on-screen. This option enables you to open multiple windows of the same document.

MDI applications provide options on the **W**indow menu for arranging document windows on the workspace. The most common options are **T**ile and **C**ascade.

The **T**ile option arranges the document windows side-by-side like tiles on a wall (see fig. 4.48).

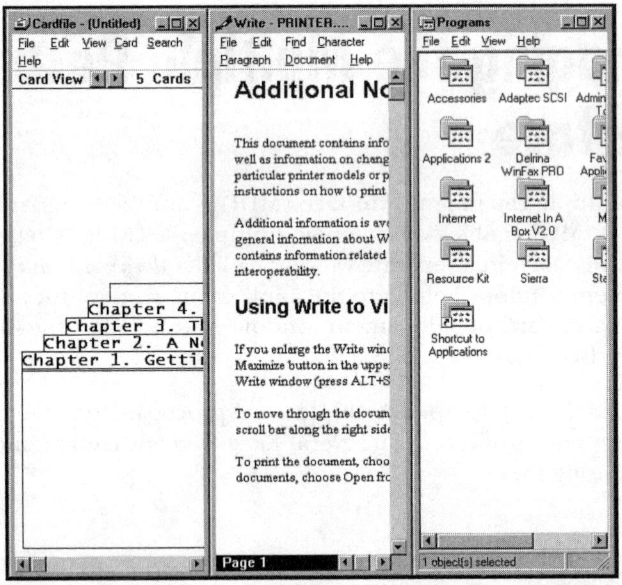

Figure 4.48

The results of the Tile command.

The **C**ascade option tumbles the document windows down the workspace from upper left to lower right (see fig. 4.49).

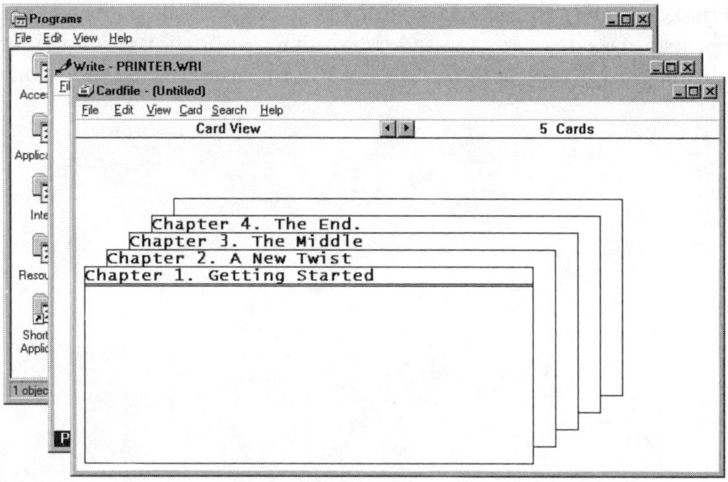

Figure 4.49

The results of the Cascade command.

Summary

When users first see Windows NT, their initial impression is how different it looks from the typical DOS, OS/2, or Unix environment. As they begin to use Windows NT, they start to comment on the differences in the way things are done. Windows NT is based on a process of selecting an object to manipulate and then performing an action. Although Windows NT can be used entirely from the keyboard, most users find it easier to use the mouse for performing many tasks. These mouse actions can be used to control the various windows on the screen.

One of the most important aspects of the Windows NT environment is its consistency between applications. The objects that are manipulated within programs are based on a small set of general item types. The most obvious item used for controlling programs is the Windows menu structure. Menu items are selected to perform tasks, to select between settings, and to display dialog boxes.

This consistency is balanced by the fact that Windows NT offers a variety of ways to perform the same task. You can select an item from a menu by using the mouse, the keyboard, or a combination of both. Most menu items (as well as items within a dialog box) have a series of accelerator keys that can be used to select them. In addition, many items have a shortcut-key combination that can be entered with a single keystroke to select the menu item.

This chapter described features that are common to all Windows NT programs. You learned that Windows NT applications have a common set of commands for performing similar tasks, which forms the basis of Windows NT's adherence to the Common User Access (CUA) standard.

These commands make it easier to use applications because you can focus on your working tasks. They also make it easier to use less-familiar applications; you can easily guess the way an application works from having worked on other applications under the same framework.

Index

Symbols

A

D

E

F

G

H

I

K

L

M

Q-R

S

U

V

W-Z